THE STATE LEGISLATURE

Politics and Practice

MALCOLM E. JEWELL

University of Kentucky

RANDOM HOUSE · New York

ACKNOWLEDGMENTS

Anyone writing in the field of comparative state government and politics is even more indebted to other students in the field than is usually the case, because his first-hand knowledge is necessarily limited to one or a few states.

Permission is gratefully acknowledged to quote several excerpts from: Duane Lockard, *New England State Politics* (Princeton: Princeton University Press, 1959). My other debts to the printed word are acknowledged in the footnotes.

In addition, a number of persons have supplied me with information and statistics more detailed or more recent than that available in their books and articles. These include: George S. Blair, William Buchanan, Leon D. Epstein, Thomas A. Flinn, John G. Grumm, Eugene E. Lee, Duane Lockard, and Allan P. Sindler. John E. Reeves of the University of Kentucky has read the manuscript and provided many helpful comments, particularly examples from his long experience with Kentucky politics. Duane Lockard has also read the manuscript and contributed valuable suggestions. The responsibility for errors of fact or judgment, of course, is mine.

Finally, I am indebted to my wife for advice and encouragement, and for her skill as a typist and patience as a proofreader.

M. E. J.

CONTENTS

CONTENTS

LIST OF TABLES

The State Legislature

ONE

INTRODUCTION

Politics is the key to understanding the American state legislature; yet the casual newspaper reader may learn more about the politics of his legislature than a student who peruses all the scholarly literature available on the subject. For a variety of reasons, the politics of state legislatures is a subject generally ignored by those writing about the legislative process.

Some studies of state legislatures have focused on such formalities of the legislative process as the length of sessions, the number and size of committees, and variations in legislative procedures. This emphasis has resulted partly from the legalistic tradition in the political science discipline and partly from the fact that gathering and summarizing precise information on such tangible questions is often easier than comparative analysis of political factors in the legislative process. Another important reason for this emphasis is that many of the available studies of individual state legislatures have been prepared primarily for the guidance of legislators and consequently have stressed the technical facts legislators must know if they are to function effectively.

Other studies have been motivated by a desire for reform. American political scientists studying state government have found many areas where reform was needed and have quite naturally concentrated their attention on those areas. The value of their studies is not disputed here. The disadvantage of reform-oriented research, however, is that it has left many areas of

3

state government unexplored while producing duplication in other areas. For example, a thorough search of periodicals and monographs would show over a hundred studies of legislative apportionment in the states and would show almost as much attention given to the problems of legislative staffing and the legislative council movement. In contrast there are only a handful of studies on the role of political parties in state legislatures.

The problems of describing the politics of state legislatures are similar to those faced by the student of comparative state politics. In both cases there are many practices that appear to defy systemizing, and it is tempting to concentrate on colorful political personalities and emphasize the uniqueness of each state's political system. In recent years, however, spurred on by V. O. Key's pioneering studies,[1] political scientists have begun to analyze state politics in a more systematic, comparative fashion. These studies suggest that a similar approach to the study of political factors in the legislative process would be possible and valuable.

The most comprehensive analysis of state legislatures to date was published in 1954 by a committee of the American Political Science Association headed by Belle Zeller.[2] It gave greater attention than most studies, to political aspects of the legislatures, but it covered only certain of these and provided few detailed examples. Some of the recent studies of state politics have provided valuable information about legislatures as a by-product. However, most of the facts necessary to provide a clear picture of the political side of the legislative process must be drawn from widely scattered and often obscure studies dealing with individual state legislatures and often giving only peripheral attention to politics.

As a starting point, it must be recognized that political patterns in American states vary widely. At one

4

extreme are the southern states still completely dominated (except in presidential politics) by a single party; at the other extreme are some highly competitive two-party states, usually the larger industrial ones. In between these two categories are some states where the apportionment system has permitted one party to retain a tight grip over at least one branch of the legislature despite alternating control over other parts of state government. If a single party dominates the state, party politics is of little importance in the legislature, where the party has no incentive to seek organizational unity. In such states the question to ask is whether some form of factionalism or regionalism serves as a substitute for partisanship in the legislature. In states with a two-party system functioning to some degree, the parties are sure to play some role in the legislature; but this role varies in nature and scope from state to state.

In states with a two-party system, political factors affect the legislature first through the electoral process. The legislator may owe his nomination and election to a political machine or to his own independent efforts. He may be elected without party opposition or he may represent a district that frequently alternates between Democratic and Republican control. These factors will affect his sensitivity to constituents and his amenability to influence by party leaders. The apportionment problem is an inescapable part of the electoral process and has major partisan implications in most states. In a two-party state it is possible but not inevitable that legislative roll calls will frequently follow party lines. For reasons that will be explored later on, there are wide variations here, with partisan considerations dominating the voting in some states and playing a peripheral role in others. In those legislatures where party is not an important factor in the roll calls, we must look for some other pattern to the voting.

Party voting may arise naturally out of the conflicts in viewpoint and the contrasting constituencies of Democratic and Republican legislators. A high level of party unity, however, must be based in part on organization and leadership. The patterns of organization need to be examined closely to determine how leaders are chosen, how caucuses operate, and what sanctions can be applied to enforce party discipline. Standing committees, traditionally the backbone of the American legislative process, may in practice be either the tools of legislative leaders or independent sources of power. They may be highly partisan or virtually nonpartisan in operation.

The state governor, like the President, has become increasingly a legislative leader in recent decades. The governor has many techniques of leadership, but there are a number of obstacles which frequently prevent a governor from acting effectively as a party leader in his relations with the legislature. Some of these obstacles, such as control of one house by the opposition party, are formidable indeed. In other cases, it appears that governors have not fully realized their potential as party leaders.

If this book has a theme, it is that the best means of making the state legislature responsible to the voters is a viable two-party system. By a responsible legislature, we mean that the voters should have a choice of candidates, should be able to understand what programs the candidates support, and should be able to defeat those candidates that have not fulfilled their promises. In the absence of a party system, the voter may have no choice of candidates or be unable to see any meaningful differences among them—often because he is unfamiliar with voting records. The two-party system creates greater responsibility not only because it usually

6

guarantees two candidates but because the parties have traditions, records, and programs that are likely to be meaningful to the voter. The parties stand for something, and in addition they provide continuity while legislative candidates come and go.

The two-party system can produce a more responsible legislature, but we have already pointed out that there are many variations and imperfections in the party systems of American states. If we are to judge the effectiveness of the legislative process in various states, it might be helpful to describe in greater detail a model of party responsibility. How should the party system work in theory in order to provide the best possible framework for a responsible legislature?

The two parties should alternate control of the state government; this does not mean constant rotation but control roughly balanced over several decades. Unless this occurs, the opposition party is likely to grow so weak that the voter's choice is more theoretical than real. At any one time, a single party should control both the governorship and the two legislative branches, but the opposition should have substantial legislative membership. If control of the state is divided, the voter may be unable to fix responsibility accurately on either party; if the opposition lacks a strong legislative voice, conflict will be muted and the voter will lose sight of the issues. Both parties should run candidates in all districts, and the legislators should seek re-election often enough so that the voters can frequently vote on a record instead of promises. The governor should run on a party platform to which legislators of his party are committed in most respects, a platform well known to the voters. Party organization and leadership in the legislature should be strong enough to create substantial (but not necessarily complete) party unity on important votes;

7

this makes it possible for the majority party to carry out its promises, and it makes the legislative candidate's party label more meaningful to the voters.

We should emphasize again the theoretical nature of this model. We will not find it duplicated exactly in the practices of any state. It simply provides a guide for our investigations. What factors are most conducive to such party responsibility? What types of states diverge most from the model? Where parties are weak, how often and how successfully do factions of some kind take their place? Once we understand more clearly how the party actually functions, we are better able to evaluate the possibilities for increased party responsibility in the legislative process.

TWO

THE ELECTION OF LEGISLATORS

I often think it's comical,
How nature always does contrive
That every boy and every gal,
That's born into the world alive,
Is either a little Liberal,
Or else a little Conservative.
                            —IOLANTHE

From the viewpoint of the legislator, political factors
first assume importance when he becomes a candidate
for election. The role played by local political organizations, the extent of alignment with a statewide party
or faction, and the degree of party competition in his
district are all electoral circumstances that may influence
his later behavior in the legislature. The individual
legislator is affected, however, not only by the circumstances of his own election but also by the statewide
political setting.

Variations in the Party Setting

In attempting to classify the varying political patterns in fifty American states, we run the risk of lump-
ing together states that differ substantially from one another. Yet we need some method of classifying states
that will distinguish clearly between those with greater
and lesser degrees of party competition. Once these
classifications—however arbitrary—have been described,
they will provide reference points for use throughout

the book. There is no single formula for defining one-party or two-party states. The time periods covered and the elective offices included by other writers vary with their purposes.[1] In order to present an up-to-date

TABLE 1a

CLASSIFICATION OF STATE LEGISLATURES ACCORDING TO DEGREE OF ONE-PARTY CONTROL (1947-1962)*

A. One-Party States: Same party controlled the governorship and both houses throughout the period and the minority representation was never over 20% in either house (all Democratic states).

Alabama	Mississippi
Arkansas	North Carolina
Florida	South Carolina
Georgia	Texas
Louisiana	Virginia

B. 1. States with One Party Dominant: Same party controlled the governorship and both houses throughout the period, but the minority sometimes exceeded 20% in the legislature.

Democratic	*Republican*
Oklahoma	New Hampshire
Tennessee	Vermont

B. 2. States with One Party Dominant: Same party controlled both houses throughout the period but did not always control the governorship.

Democratic	*Republican*
Arizona	Iowa
Kentucky	Kansas
Maryland	Maine
West Virginia	New York
	North Dakota

* Alaska and Hawaii are omitted from Tables 1a and 1b because of their brief terms as states, and Nebraska and Minnesota are omitted because they have nonpartisan legislatures. The time period is 1946-1961 for states with off-year elections: Kentucky, New Jersey, Virginia, Mississippi, and Louisiana.

CLASSIFICATION OF STATE LEGISLATURES ACCORDING TO DEGREE
OF TWO-PARTY COMPETITION (1947-1962)

State	Senate			House			Governor-ship	
	D	R	Tie	D	R	Tie	D	R

C. 1. Limited Two-Party States: Same party controlled both houses throughout most of the period and the governorship at least half of the time.

State	D	R	Tie	D	R	Tie	D	R
South Dakota	2	14	—	0	16	—	2	14
Wisconsin	0	16	—	2	14	—	4	12
Missouri	14	2	—	12	4	—	16	0
Illinois	4	12	—	0	16	—	6	10
Indiana	2	14	—	4	12	—	6	10
New Mexico	16	0	—	14	2	—	8	8
Wyoming	0	16	—	2	12	2	8	8
New Jersey	0	16	—	4	12	—	8	8

C. 2. Limited Two-Party States: Same party controlled both houses throughout most of the period but usually not the governorship.

State	D	R	Tie	D	R	Tie	D	R
Michigan	0	16	—	0	14	2	14	2
Ohio	4	12	—	4	12	—	12	4

C. 3. Limited Two-Party States: Two houses controlled by different parties during most of the period.

State	D	R	Tie	D	R	Tie	D	R
Nevada	16	0	—	0	16	—	8	8
Rhode Island	4	6	6	16	0	—	14	2
Connecticut	10	6	—	2	14	—	10	6
Massachusetts	4	10	2	12	4	—	8	8

D. Two-Party States: Neither party had dominant legislative control, and party control of legislature approximated control of governorship.

State	D	R	Tie	D	R	Tie	D	R
Pennsylvania	0	14	2	6	10	—	8	8
Idaho	6	10	—	2	14	—	6	10
California	4	10	2	4	12	—	4	12
Oregon	4	10	2	6	10	—	2	14
Montana	6	10	—	8	8	—	4	12
Washington	8	6	2	12	4	—	8	8
Utah	8	8	—	6	8	2	2	14
Colorado	6	10	—	8	8	—	12	4
Delaware	10	6	—	8	8	—	6	10

picture of the legislatures, we have chosen the sixteen-year period, 1947-1962, have eliminated presidential and congressional elections, and at the state level have focused primarily on the legislatures.

Tables 1a and 1b indicate both the wide variety in political patterns and the scarcity of states that approach the model of two-party competition. In the first ten southern states (A.), interparty competition may be described as a nonexistent factor. In several of these legislative bodies a Republican has not been seen for years. In others there are a handful of Republicans, usually representing pockets of Republican strength such as those in the Blue Ridge region of North Carolina. In the next category of four states (B. 1), the minority party has been strong enough in the legislature, at least during some sessions, to give the party factor some relevance if not necessarily much importance. The next category of states (B. 2) differs from the preceding one not only because the minority party usually has stronger representation in the legislature but, more importantly, because it sometimes controls the governorship. Normally the minority representation is strong in at least one branch of the legislature when that party elects a governor. The fact of alternating gubernatorial control provides both parties with some incentive to maintain sufficient unity to develop a party record. The states in this category vary considerably. Kansas, Iowa, and Maine, for example, had been one-sided Republican states until recent Democratic breakthroughs in the gubernatorial contests. Kentucky and Maryland are examples of states where long-term Democratic control has been interrupted occasionally by Republican governors. New York, on the other hand, has vigorous two-party competition in gubernatorial contests but has a legislature regularly controlled by the Republicans.

The states in categories C. 1 and C. 2 are ones that

17

would be generally thought of as two-party states, yet in all of them, during the postwar period, one party has controlled both legislative branches at least three-quarters of the time. In all but two of these states (Missouri and New Mexico) the predominant legislative control has been Republican. South Dakota and Wisconsin resemble several states in the preceding category (B. 2); the difference is that in these two states the emerging Democratic party has on one occasion captured one house as well as the governorship. In Illinois, Indiana, Wyoming, New Jersey, Michigan, and Ohio there has been tight Republican control over the legislature, but the governorship has either been rather evenly divided or, in the last two cases, has usually been under Democratic control. The states in category C. 3 are likewise two-party states, but are ones in which each party has developed a hold over one branch of the legislature that usually remains constant despite the outcome of the gubernatorial race. In most of the states in category C, partisan factors significantly influence legislative developments, but the governor (particularly a Democrat) often faces an opposition majority in at least one branch of the legislature.

The states in category D most nearly approach the model of two-party competition; in these legislatures partisan influences may be expected to be considerable. Even here a quick examination of the table shows several cases where one branch of the legislature frequently has a party majority opposing the governor. Category D also contains variations. Some of the states have had long records of close two-party competition. In Pennsylvania, California, and Oregon, however, the Democrats have only recently emerged into a strongly competitive position.

Anyone who tries to classify the state legislatures in this fashion must recognize the arbitrary and artificial nature of the process. Party competition should actually be measured by a dual standard: the historical pattern and the present situation. In a state like New York or Ohio, long-established two-party competition makes the legislative process highly partisan even during a session when one party has a large majority in the legislature. In a state like Wisconsin or California, partisanship in the legislature has a newly acquired importance because of recent Democratic gains. The roots of partisanship are different in these two pairs of states; both will bear fruit, but perhaps of different varieties. The habits of party organization and party voting may be acquired quickly but could be lost just as quickly.

Today there are probably more state legislatures where politics is based on the competition of closely balanced parties than at any other time in modern American history. Outside of the South and a few Border States, the Republicans in the past have frequently dominated state legislatures, even in states where the governorship often changed hands. During the early days of the New Deal the Democrats gained legislative control in a number of states, but the party was seldom well enough organized to maintain this control beyond one or two sessions. The revival of Democratic strength that occurred in the late 1950's was based much more solidly on organizational strength. The consequence has been not only the capture of a large number of governorships but the gaining of legislative control in many states where the party had long been a minority.

Increased party competition in the states does not necessarily reduce divided government, however, and may actually make it more likely. In his book, *American State Politics*, V. O. Key has shown what a familiar phenomenon this was in American state government from 1931 through 1952. Bringing his figures up to date through 1962, we find that only fourteen states had no divided government during the thirty-two-year period. These are the same fourteen in our categories A and B. 1, the solid one-party states. There were nine states with from two to eight years of divided government, and in most of these, one party controlled the legislature all or most of the time. There were seventeen more states with divided government ten to sixteen years, and six more states with divided government eighteen to twenty-four years out of the total thirty-two-year period.[2] Even if the more recent time period, 1947-1962, is selected, there is no state with some alternation in gubernatorial or legislative control that has escaped divided government throughout the period.

A more accurate understanding of divided government can be obtained by exploring the circumstances under which it has arisen in thirty-two states (excluding the fourteen in categories A and B. 1 and those with nonpartisan legislatures). In Key's words, "Although the rain supposedly falls on the wicked and the virtuous alike, Republican governors in our thirty-two states had much less of whatever grief comes from dealing with an opposition legislature than did Democratic chief executives." Key's figures show that, as a result of the elections from 1930 through 1950, Democratic governors had to face an opposition majority in at least one branch of the legislature 51 per cent of the time; the figure for Republican governors was 18 per cent.[3] Since Key wrote, this has continued to be a frequent problem for Democratic governors and has become increasingly one for Republicans. As a result of the five elections, 1952-1960, in these same thirty-two states, Democratic governors encountered opposition control in at least part of the legislature 55 per cent of the time and Republicans 39 per cent of the time. It is also generally true that the larger a governor's electoral majority, the better his chances of winning a legislative majority.

There are several explanations for divided government. In states where one party is usually dominant, the minority party may be too poorly organized and too short of good candidates to make vigorous and persistent efforts at winning the legislature. When that minority party wins the governorship on the strength of a particularly popular candidate or the weakness of the other party's candidate, the party is often too weak to capture a legislative majority. This was the experience of Democratic parties in the late 1950's that elected governors in states like Maine, South Dakota, Kansas, and Iowa. In some of these cases the governor's coat tails may be sufficient to win a majority in one house, but this may be lost during the second half of his four-year term.[4]

The other major cause of divided government is the system of representation. Most familiar is a constitutional formula for apportioning at least one legislative branch that discriminates against urban areas. In states like Connecticut, Rhode Island, New Jersey, and Michigan this has usually prevented Democratic governors from having complete legislative majorities, while in Maryland it has worked to the disadvantage of a Republican governor. In both New York and Massachusetts the Democrats have been handicapped by two other factors. Republican legislatures have gerrymandered the legislative districts, designing them so as to help Republican candidates. In both those states, and some others, the Democratic vote has been so heavily concentrated in metropolitan areas and so thinly spread throughout the rest of the state that, under the single-member district system, it has been difficult to gain Democratic majorities in the legislature. The problems of representation have political ramifications that require more extended treatment in the pages that follow.

Although the proportion of Democratic governors lacking a party majority in the legislature has remained steady for several decades, the circumstances have changed as a result of Democratic victories at the polls. In a number of normally Republican states the Democrats have elected governors during the late 1950's for the first time since the Depression, but have usually not elected legislatures. On the other hand, in states like Rhode Island, Massachusetts, and Connecticut, recent Democratic landslides have sometimes been great enough to produce a complete legislative majority, for the first time in years or even decades.

Why has divided government become more frequent in Republican administrations? In the Southwest (Arizona, New Mexico, and Nevada) and the Border State of Maryland, the Republicans have encountered the familiar problems of long-term minority parties winning the governorship. In several other states the revival of Democratic strength appears to have produced Democratic majorities that persisted in the legislature after the governorship had been recaptured by the Republican party. Divided government might appear if the Republicans should capture the governorship in states like Virginia and North Carolina, where Republican voters are concentrated in a few areas, some of which are under-represented; this has been the pattern during the few Republican administrations in Kentucky.

Techniques of Legislative Apportionment

Apportionment is one of the few aspects of the legislative process that has been adequately studied by political scientists, and we need only survey those parts of the problem that affect political parties in the legislature. The essence of the apportionment problem in American state legislatures is simple. We live in a

17

rapidly changing society with a highly mobile population. Legislative control by representatives of rural areas,
which was assured as long as the population was overwhelmingly rural, was threatened by the growth of
modern cities and later of metropolitan centers. This
was not merely a clash between the inhabitants of
farms and cities: "The rise of cities in the nineteenth
century caused the emergence of a large class of prop-
erty-less laborers, whose enfranchisement alarmed men
of substance, both rural and urban." [5] The cities were
often populated heavily by new immigrants, whose votes
were to some extent controlled by political bosses. The
inhabitants of farms and small towns distrusted the
city folk and saw no reason to surrender control of the
state to them, if it could be avoided. The strongest
resistance developed in those states where a single
metropolitan area (or perhaps a pair of them) at-
tained or approached a numerical majority of the state's
population. In some cases the conflict was intensified by
the fact that the dominant political party (often Republican) drew its greatest support from the farms and
small towns while the minority party was stronger in
urban centers.

There are essentially three ways in which a rural
group might maintain its control over the legislature.
Since the responsibility for reapportionment is usually
delegated by the state constitution to the legislature,
the majority group in the legislature could simply do
nothing. A second strategy would be to secure constitutional standards for apportionment that would preserve
rural control in one or both branches of the legislature.
A third method would be to pass redistricting bills from
time to time that gave proportionately greater representation to rural than to urban areas and perhaps
favored a particular party. These techniques have sometimes been used in combination. In Illinois, for ex-

ample, there was no reapportionment of the state legislature from 1901 until 1955, to the distinct disadvantage of Chicago and the other parts of Cook County. When reapportionment was finally achieved, downstate groups were able to exact a high price for it: a new constitutional provision guaranteed periodic reapportionment of the House on a population basis but established a Senate apportionment that assured a numerical majority to the downstate area.

Though apportionment systems vary greatly in the different states, the legislative districts are always based on existing units of government, usually the counties but sometimes cities and towns. Sometimes all counties (or cities and towns) are equally represented, but the apportionment generally bears some relationship to the population of these units and consequently is supposed to vary as population changes.

Most state constitutions require periodic reapportionment of one or both houses and delegate this responsibility to the legislature. Though the language of the constitution usually makes this reapportionment mandatory (normally after the federal census), legislative bodies have frequently delayed for many years. The example of Illinois has already been cited. Although (or perhaps because) the Tennessee constitution provides for almost no distortion in the population principle for apportionment, the legislative seats in that state were last apportioned in 1903, and House districts there vary from 3,500 to 79,000 in population. There are several other states with apportionments at least thirty years out of date. In the last few decades, on the average only about half of the states have reapportioned their legislatures during the ten years following each census, although the proportion was higher after 1950.

One of the consequences of long delays in reapportionment, of course, is that substantial inequalities may develop even in that section of a state which appears to hold the upper hand by virtue of the old apportionment. It should be noted that legislators often avoid their duty of reapportionment not only to avoid weakening their party or region but also to avoid hurting their own political futures (or those of their colleagues) by revising district lines. In some cases where reapportionment will have relatively minor political results, this personal reason for delay may be the most important one.

It may seem absurd to expect a legislative body to carry out an apportionment operation on itself promptly and accurately. Partly as a consequence of long delays in the past, several states have given a non-legislative official or commission either complete authority to reapportion or authority to do so if the legislature fails to act in a given period after the census. One of the advantages of such a delegation of authority is that these officials are clearly subject to mandamus action of the courts if they fail to fulfill their responsibilities.

While the courts in various states have proved willing to review reapportionment legislation and to reverse laws deemed to violate constitutional provisions, the courts have traditionally refused to order legislative action on apportionment, insisting that the remedy for such inaction lies at the polls. In the past the federal courts have provided no remedy for citizens who claimed that rights guaranteed by the federal constitution were being violated by legislatures that refused to reapportion. Decisions by federal district courts in Hawaii and Minnesota in 1956 and 1958, however, indicated that the federal judiciary may be prepared to offer judicial relief to the victims of outdated apportionment at the state level.[6] The U. S. Supreme Court has recently agreed to hear a case growing out of six decades without reapportionment in Tennessee.

In twenty American states the initiative offers one other potential means of overcoming legislative inaction. In California, Arkansas, Michigan, and Oregon constitutional amendments altering the apportionment system have been initiated by the voters and approved; in Washington and Oregon statutory initiatives on apportionment have been passed. Through the initiative process the voters could, as they did in Arkansas in 1936, take the power of apportionment away from the legislature and place it in other hands.

Rural elements in the states have frequently sought to protect their privileged position in legislative apportionment through constitutional provisions. Since it is difficult to amend most constitutions, at least with respect to controversial matters, this is a particularly effective technique. There are a variety of devices that have been incorporated into constitutions to serve this purpose, and they apply to about two-thirds of the legislative bodies. In a sense the most rigid is the device of writing a precise apportionment into the constitution. The Delaware Constitution in 1897 made such an apportionment among the three counties in the state; as a consequence, a county that has grown to over two-thirds of the state's population has only about 40 per cent of the legislative seats. A fixed apportionment system was introduced for the Michigan Senate in 1952, as part of a compromise that provided an enforceable method for periodic apportionment of the House. Some of the most extreme inequalities arise in the several states that permit each county, or in some cases each city or town, to have one and only one member in one branch of the legislature (usually the Senate). The one-senator counties in New Jersey vary in size from

48,000 to 923,000. In Vermont the members of the House represent towns and cities varying in population from 49 up to 35,531.

A common constitutional provision is one which limits the population principle in apportionment by favoring smaller units, limiting the larger ones, or both. Frequently every county is given at least one member in the lower house, and in a state with many counties the population principle may be largely negated. Iowa, for example, has ninety-nine counties and is limited by its constitution to a lower house of 108 seats; thus only the nine largest counties have two members in the House, and the representation of the smallest county is eighteen times as great as that of the largest. Another technique is to limit the apportionment of the largest units either in percentage terms, or in the number of representatives, or by limiting any county to one member while smaller counties are grouped together into districts. In Florida this has produced Senate districts ranging in size from 10,000 to 935,000. Some states combine these two approaches by limiting the larger units and favoring the smaller ones. In the Florida House, for example, each county has one member, the five largest are permitted three, and the eighteen next largest may have two members; the resulting districts vary from less than 2,900 to over 300,000.

Some state constitutions that largely follow the population principle and some that include restrictions already discussed also vary the ratio used in the apportionment process. The ratio is normally found by dividing the state's population by the number of seats. In some cases a county may have one representative with only half the normal ratio, while some states have a ratio that gradually increases as the number of seats given to a county grows.

The techniques for achieving unequal apportionment

are varied, but in a state with rapidly growing urban areas any one of the foregoing may serve quite effectively to preserve rural power in the legislature.

If the constitution provides for apportionment based largely on population and if the legislature acts with considerable regularity, there is still no guarantee that the resulting apportionment may provide equality. In Wisconsin, where population is the constitutional standard for apportionment, the 1957 apportionment act created Assembly districts varying from 19,000 to 51,000 (based on the 1950 population); under similar conditions the 1957 apportionment act in Washington created Senate districts ranging from 22,000 to 128,000.

In the absence of constitutional limitations, the legislature may create unequal districts in order to favor rural areas or to assist one political party; where one party is predominantly urban, of course, the two motives may be intermingled. A legislature may establish districts that are roughly equal in size but that favor one party because of the way in which district lines are drawn. This is the practice commonly known as gerrymandering. The exact tactics may vary, but the strategy is uniform. One party can sometimes divide a center of opposition strength among several districts so that the opposition has a majority in none; alternatively, it may concentrate as much of the opposition strength as possible into a single district in order to make the other districts safe for the majority. Districts may be gerrymandered to help particular factions of a party or even individual legislators. Districts may, of course, be created that are both gerrymandered and unequal in size. The legislature may also have political reasons for providing multi-member rather than single-member districts in the state; for example, it would be easier for a Democratic legislature to eliminate Republican legislators from a large urban center having twenty representa-

23

tives if it created five large, multi-member districts than if it used twenty single-member districts in the urban center. Normally in a multi-member district the voters will choose a full slate of legislative candidates belonging to the majority party.

The Political Consequences of Malapportionment

There is no doubt that the systems of apportionment currently used in many of the states discriminate against the major urban centers. It is not unusual for the three or four largest cities or counties to have representation in one or both houses that is one-half, one-third, or even less of their proportion of state population. It is more difficult to measure what effect this has on party control of the legislature. Where one party dominates the state, this question may be irrelevant; it is most relevant in states where the apportionment system has permitted one party to hold a majority in one house despite a landslide for the other party in the other house and in votes for the governorship.

There may be several reasons why one party has a smaller percentage of seats in the legislature than its proportion of the vote for governor or for legislative seats. Let us assume that the Democrats elect a governor in a northern state for the first time in a decade, but fail to elect a majority in the legislature. The cause may be organizational; the party may have failed to run candidates, or at least well-known, experienced candidates, for all the legislative seats. Many voters may have split their tickets and voted for a popular Democratic gubernatorial candidate and Republican legislators. If, for whatever reason, a *minority* of the total votes cast for legislative candidates went to the Democrats, the normal workings of the single-member district system would produce an even smaller percentage of elected Democratic legislators.

If the Democrats won a *majority* of the votes cast for legislative candidates, their failure to win a legislative majority is not proof of unequal apportionment. Democratic voters may be highly concentrated in one or two major urban centers, where some of their legislative votes but not their gubernatorial votes are wasted. To take a hypothetical example, let us assume that a state has one million voters, located in 100 legislative districts of 10,000 voters each. In two metropolitan centers there are 400,000 voters and 40 districts. The Democrats elect a governor, winning 300,000 out of 400,000 metropolitan votes and 250,000 of the remaining 600,000. No voter splits his ticket, but in spite of a total vote of 550,000, the Democrats fail to carry the legislature. They elect representatives in 35 of 40 metropolitan districts, usually by large majorities which waste votes, and in only 10 of the remaining 60 districts, though they often win 40 or 45 per cent of the legislative vote in these areas. In states that use multi-member districts, the winner-takes-all factor is maximized because no system of proportional representation is used in the districts. In a district where the voters are to choose four representatives, the stronger party usually wins all four seats. In the example just cited, the Democrats would probably have won all 40 of the metropolitan representatives and none of the others if districts with three or four members each had been common.

In practice it is common to find states where a minority party is under-represented in the legislature for several reasons: some of its local organizations are too weak to run strong candidates, the constitutional apportionment system favors the other party, and the apportionment law is more than a decade old and when drawn created somewhat unequal districts with some degree of gerrymandering. These factors may counterbalance each other, or they may all operate to the advantage of a single party. Whatever the case, it is impossible to measure accurately and separately the impact of each factor on the number of Democrats and Republicans elected.

For the reasons we have discussed, divided government in the states cannot always be blamed on the apportionment system, but the political effects of malapportionment can best be demonstrated by examples of divided government. Connecticut is a good example. It is a highly competitive two-party state in which Democrats have served as governors during twenty-four years in this century. Though the Democrats have frequently won a Senate majority, in 1958 they won their first House majority since 1876. Because it is a highly competitive state with strong organizations and because both parties generally run candidates for virtually every House seat, the apportionment system can be pinpointed as the cause of Republican majorities in the House. In 1954 Democrat Abraham Ribicoff was elected governor with less than 51 per cent of the vote. During the next four years he faced Republican House majorities of 184 to 92 and 249 to 30 in the two sessions. His electoral margin, like that of most of his Democratic predecessors, was small, but when he won by an impressive 62 per cent majority in 1958 he had a House majority of only three, which evaporated in the 1960 election. The House apportionment greatly favors the small towns, which are the main source of Republican strength in Connecticut. In the 1954 election, for example, 101 towns, each under 5,000 population, had 11 per cent of the state's population and elected 143 of the 279 House members, 119 of them Republicans. Four cities, with 30 per cent of the population, had eight representatives, all Democrats.[7]

26

Michigan provides one of the clearest examples of an apportionment system that shapes the politics of a state. Since the 1948 election the state has had Democratic governors continuously, elected by margins sometimes very bare and sometimes as high as 56 per cent, but (excluding a tie in the House in 1959-1960) there has not been a Democratic majority in either house. Both parties are well organized and run candidates in all or virtually all legislative districts. Democratic strength is heavily concentrated in the industrial centers, notably Wayne County (Detroit), where 45 per cent of the state's Democratic votes for governor were cast in 1960. This concentration of Democratic voters in the under-represented areas has cost the party control of the legislature.

Under the 1952 apportionment compromise, the Michigan Senate districts are fixed by the constitution; Wayne County has seven out of thirty-four. In the 1960 election the Democratic candidate won 50.6 per cent of the gubernatorial vote, but Democratic candidates for the thirty-four Senate contests won *more*, 52.1 per cent of the vote. This gave the Democrats only twelve seats out of thirty-four, as many as the party has won in recent years. In the House, smaller counties are over-represented because they need only one-half a ratio for the first representative. In the 1961-1962 legislature, twenty of the twenty-six House districts with less than a full ratio are represented by Republicans.

In general the apportionment system has had the most obvious political effect in states meeting these conditions: rural counties are greatly over-represented in at least one house, Democratic strength is heavily concentrated in the large cities, and the Democrats have won the governorship some or most of the time in recent years. Illinois, Ohio, and New Jersey are other good examples of states where this has been true.[8] In

27

New York, where Democratic governors have normally had to contend with Republican legislatures, the disparity appears to result primarily from gerrymandering and the drawing of unequal districts, as well as the heavy concentration of Democratic voters in a few metropolitan areas. In some states the under-representation of Republican suburbs may tend to offset the under-representation of Democratic cities. There has been evidence of such a trend in states like Illinois, New York, and Pennsylvania.

There are several states, and the number is likely to increase, where the apportionment system works to the disadvantage of the Republican party. In some traditionally Democratic states where there is relatively little Republican strength in rural areas, the Republicans are dependent on growing strength in the urban and suburban areas to overcome their minority status. In such cases malapportionment helps to maintain Democratic dominance of the legislature. An example is Maryland, where Theodore McKeldin served as Republican governor from 1951 through 1958 with a Democratic legislature; in the lower house the Republicans had only 20 to 30 per cent of the members. Organizational factors were one cause, but the under-representation of suburban areas hurt the Republicans also. At present Baltimore City is slightly under-represented in the House; it usually elects a full slate of Democrats. The three largest suburban counties (outside Baltimore and Washington) have 250,000 more people than Baltimore but together elect half as many representatives in each branch; two of these three counties elected predominantly Republicans at the height of Republican strength under McKeldin.

In several of the southwestern states, notably Arizona and New Mexico, malapportionment has resulted both from constitutional provisions and from the slowness of

28

legislatures to give new representation to the mush-rooming urban centers. Republicans in Arizona have been handicapped by habitual Democratic registration and organizational weakness, and also by the Senate apportionment system. There are only two senators for each Arizona county, and the counties vary in population from 7,736 to 663,510; the largest county has half the state's population, and the second largest has 20 per cent. In 1958 the Republican plurality in the largest county provided the margin of victory for the governor, and the two largest counties provided all but one of the twenty-five Republican House seats and the party's only Senate seat.

If and when the Republicans begin to persuade the presidential Republican voters in southern states to vote for state Republican candidates, their efforts will be handicapped by malapportionment. Already in Florida the few Republican representatives come primarily from a few large urban centers that are under-represented.

Kentucky illustrates how a minority party may be handicapped by inequalities that are not evident on the surface. In that state the larger urban centers are under-represented, particularly in the House. Since both parties have urban and rural centers of strength, the malapportionment has no immediate and obvious political consequences. The Republicans usually win about one-fourth of the legislative seats, mostly in rural areas. On those infrequent occasions when the Republicans elect a governor, however, they usually win additional seats, primarily in the urban centers where the party organization is strong and regularly runs candidates. If these urban centers were adequately represented, the Republicans might be able to win a legislative majority in those years in which they elect a governor.

In a number of the states malapportionment weakens

29

the two-party system in one of two ways. In closely competitive states it often helps to prevent one of the parties from exercising full executive and legislative control when it wins a majority of votes in gubernatorial and legislative contests. In some of the states dominated in the past by one party, it handicaps an emerging minority party because a governor of that party may be unable to make an impressive record if the legislature is controlled (sometimes overwhelmingly) by the opposition.

The apportionment system may act as a deterrent to a minority party, discouraging it from contesting some of the legislative seats aggressively. It is most important politically when it produces divided government. If a governor cannot command a legislative majority, and particularly if the apportionment system makes it unlikely that he will in the future, he is forced to bargain with the opposition party to enact his program. The result may be a stalemate, as in Michigan where the Democratic governor and Republican legislature could not agree on the form of additional taxes. The result may be irresponsibility, as in Rhode Island and Connecticut where the two parties, often controlling different houses, tossed the question of a direct primary law back and forth for years. The result in many states is that the governor can achieve some of his program if he pays a high enough price in patronage or public works projects to members of the opposition party.

Compromise is the essence of democratic government, and proponents of politically divided government have argued that it forces moderation and respect for minority rights on the elected majority. This may be true, but compromise in divided state governments is too often simply bargaining for favors, organized bilateral logrolling. In divided government the compromises are too often reached in secret, smoke-filled rooms during the hectic closing hours of a legislative session, and the public knows little and understands less about the price paid for legislative results. The most valid criticism of an apportionment system that encourages divided government is that it breeds irresponsibility. Both parties can make promises that need not be kept because the other party can be blamed for inaction. The apportionment system does not permit the voters in some states to choose clearly between a Democratic and a Republican government, nor does it permit them to judge intelligently the actions of their elected officials.

One of the least understood implications of malapportionment is its effect on the *internal* structure of parties, which sometimes discourages growth of a stronger two-party system. For example, the frequent Republican majorities in the Rhode Island Senate, in the face of normal Democratic majorities in the state's voting, have handicapped Republican efforts to overcome their minority status. The Senate Republicans, representing small towns, hold deeply conservative views; the record they make in the Senate is not calculated to win the urban votes needed if the party is to capture the governorship with any frequency. Individual Republican senators have sometimes voted with the Democratic majority, not to establish a more liberal party record, but for favors and patronage. These Republican senators often have more to gain from dealing with the Democratic administration than from trying to elect a Republican administration.[9] A minority party is always tempted to settle for crumbs from the majority's table; this temptation can be fatal to a two-party system, and the temptation is greater if the apportionment system has given the minority party an outpost in one branch of the legislature.

The Border State of Kentucky is very different from urbanized Rhode Island, but its Republican party has a somewhat similar problem. Republican strength is growing most rapidly in the urban and suburban areas, where the party must win more votes to capture the governorship. Republicans in the legislature represent primarily rural counties with shrinking populations, however, and the programs they advance are designed primarily to win the rural voter. These Republicans have formed alliances with Democratic governors, most recently in the 1958 session, when the governor was beset by dissension in his own party. The Republican legislators can win favors from the administration, but cannot thereby establish a record on which a Republican gubernatorial candidate can run.

As the nation becomes more urbanized and as the Democrats consolidate their recent gains in many northern states, the Republicans may become increasingly handicapped by apportionment systems favoring rural areas. Republicans need urban votes to elect a governor, but the rural wing of the party is proportionately much stronger than the urban wing in the legislature of states like Ohio, Michigan, New York and Connecticut. In New York, Republican legislators have often appeared conscious of the need to establish a record liberal enough for their gubernatorial candidate's campaign, but this is probably not typical of Republican performance in other states.

In one-party states, notably in the South, the over-representation of rural areas in the legislature has clearly given an advantage to the rural wing of the dominant party. In Louisiana the Long organization was originally strongest in the over-represented rural areas, particularly in the northern part of the state. In Florida the apportionment system has strengthened the hand of rural, conservative Democrats with the most extreme segregationist views. Conservative Democrats benefit from the moderate over-representation of rural areas in Texas. In the Alabama legislature the 1906 apportionment favors the black-belt counties, where segregationist sentiment is generally strongest.[10]

An outstanding and unusual example of the effects of apportionment in a one-party state is provided by Georgia. The Democratic primary there is determined by the county-unit system; each county has twice as many votes as its seats in the legislature, and they are cast as a block. In the legislature, and consequently in county-unit voting, the rural counties are over-represented. A candidate can be nominated for statewide office with a minority of popular votes. Moreover, in Georgia party rules require rotation of senators among counties in a senatorial district and permit only the citizens of the candidates' home county to vote in the primary. Gordon Baker cites the example of an urban county comprising 85 per cent of a senatorial district but able to vote in only one-third of the senatorial primaries because it is joined with two small rural counties.[11]

In both two-party and one-party states, party organizations—state committees, conventions, and other groups—are frequently organized on the basis of legislative districts. This can be an important and little recognized way of maintaining disproportionate rural influence over the parties.

Party Competition for Legislative Seats

One important characteristic of a state dominated by a single party is that the minority party is likely to be weak organizationally, so weak in some legislative districts that it runs no candidate at all. Obviously under these circumstances the voter has no choice at the polls, at least in the general election. A newly elected governor of the minority party often faces an opposition legislature partly because in many districts his party has so seldom run candidates that it is unable to find a candidate—or at least a strong one—to run for the legislature.

Before trying to measure how often there are gaps in legislative contests, we must explain more carefully the election systems used for the legislature. The best recent survey of district systems was conducted in 1954 by Maurice Klain, who found that 88 per cent of the Senate seats in state legislatures were in single-member districts; the rest were in districts of two, three, or four seats. While single-member districts prevailed, there were only nine states where this was the only type used. Of the House seats, 55 per cent were in single-member districts; most of the multi-member districts had two, three, or four seats, but there were districts with twelve, fifteen, sixteen, or seventeen seats. Legislators from multi-member districts constituted a majority of the lower house in twenty-one states and a minority in fifteen; all were chosen from single-member districts in twelve states.[12]

We have already noted that the majority party in any area benefits from multi-member districts and that Democratic gains from such a system sometimes tend to counterbalance the party loss resulting from underrepresentation of the urban areas. In a district electing three legislators, for example, the voters have three votes and usually (though not always) elect a full slate of Democrats or a full slate of Republicans. Exceptions occur only if the parties are very closely balanced or if one candidate is much more popular than others on his ticket. In an urban multi-member district where one party predominates, the minority party frequently runs a few candidates but not as many as it is entitled to in the district. As a consequence all the voters in the area have some choice of candidates, while if the area were broken up into single-member districts the minority party might fail to run candidates in all of them. On the other hand, in a multi-member district the minority party may make less effort to run a full slate if it has some candidates on the ballot.

The only state which uses its multi-seat districts to provide minority representation is Illinois, which operates under a cumulative voting system with three-seat districts for the House. The Illinois voter may give all three of his votes to one candidate, give a vote and a half each to two, give a single vote to each of three, or give two to one and one to another. Under this system in most districts the stronger party elects only two of the three representatives. This system virtually guarantees a strong minority party in the legislature, but it encourages party committees to run only as many candidates as they are likely to elect, in order not to waste votes. If the minority party, for example, ran two candidates and the votes were evenly divided among them, the majority party might be able to elect all three candidates though it had only two-thirds of the vote. A study by George S. Blair showed that between 1944 and 1954 the two parties together nominated only three candidates in half of the district elections. In twenty-two of the fifty-one districts this practice occurred throughout the period; in other words, the voters in these districts had no choice at all, over a twelve-year period. In Illinois the low level of competition for lower house seats is a direct consequence of the cumulative voting system. It should be noted that the voters sometimes have a choice in the primaries, however.[13]

Relatively little attention has been paid to the question of legislative candidates who run without opposition. The questions we must ask first are how often this occurs and what causes it. Then we will consider whether primary competition is a frequent and effec-

TABLE 2

PERCENTAGE OF LEGISLATIVE SEATS CONTESTED
BY BOTH PARTIES*

One-Party States and States with One Party Dominant				Limited and Complete Two-Party States			
State Legislature		%	Years	State Legislature		%	Years
A.				**C. 1.**			
North Carolina	S	41	1952, 1956-60	Indiana	H	95	1948
North Carolina	H	46	1952, 1956-60	Missouri	S	76	1958
				Missouri	H	66	1958
B. 1.				Wisconsin	S	84	1946-56
New Hampshire	S	88	1960	Wisconsin	H	85	1946-56
New Hampshire	H	41	1950	**C. 2.**			
B. 2.				Michigan	S	100	1958-60
Kentucky	S	46	1947-57	Michigan	H	98	1958-60
Kentucky	H	40	1947-57	Ohio	H	82	1948
Maryland	S	89	1954-58				
Maryland	H	88	1954-58	**C. 3.**			
				Connecticut	H	99	1954
West Virginia	S	100	1958				
West Virginia	H	95	1958	Massachusetts	S	78	1954
				Massachusetts	H	72	1954
Iowa	S	95	1958				
Iowa	H	94	1958	Rhode Island	S	100	1952-56
				Rhode Island	H	100	1952-56
Maine	S	85	1954-56				
Maine	H	79	1954-56	**D.**			
				California	S	45	1956
New York	S	100	1958	California	H	78	1956
New York	H	100	1958				
				Oregon	S	80	1958
				Oregon	H	95	1958

* Grouped according to degree of party competition. See Tables 1a and 1b.

tive substitute for two-party competition. Table 2 provides some examples of states having varying degrees of party competition for legislative seats.[14] The figures are percentages of the maximum possible competition;

in the case of multi-member districts, a full slate of candidates is required for a 100 per cent figure, and if one party ran only two candidates for four seats, this would mean that only 50 per cent of the seats were contested.

We can start by testing the assumption that more seats are contested in states with close two-party competition. In the southern states where the legislatures are almost completely Democratic, there seems to be relatively little party competition for the legislature, though North Carolina is one exception. Outside the Solid South, however, Table 2 shows that there is no clear and simple correlation between party competition on the statewide level and the frequency of election contests. Kentucky and West Virginia are rather similar Border States where the Democrats regularly have comfortable legislative majorities; in Kentucky less than half of the seats are contested, while in West Virginia nearly all of them are. In California and Oregon, both closely competitive states in recent years, there are more uncontested elections than in Michigan and Connecticut, both states apportioned to provide consistent majorities to a single party in one house. Close statewide competition is only one of the factors causing contested elections.

Legislative contests are more likely to be found where there are strong local party organizations. It is primarily the responsibility of the party organization to assure that candidates file for legislative contests; the absence of candidates indicates a breakdown in party responsibility. A party that has long been in a minority throughout the state is likely to have serious organizational weaknesses in many localities; yet even a strong party accustomed to frequent statewide victories may have local gaps in organizational strength.

What factors affect the strength of local party or-

37

ganizations? V. O. Key has advanced the theory that the growth of the direct primary for statewide and local nominations has weakened local party organizations, particularly in the minority party, by depriving them of a major function: complete responsibility for nominations. He has pointed out that the percentage of uncontested nominations grew sharply in several states after the direct primary was adopted.[15] If this assumption is true, a major reason why virtually all seats in Rhode Island and Connecticut are contested is that in both states the direct primary has been adopted only recently and the parties have continued to endorse candidates who run subject to only occasional challenge in the primaries. From 1952 through 1956, for example, only 19 per cent of the Democrats and 9 per cent of the Republicans endorsed by their respective parties were challenged in the Rhode Island legislative primaries.[16] In Indiana, though primaries determine local candidates, statewide candidates are chosen by conventions, and therefore the local party units have a reason for maintaining their vitality. In that state there is two-party competition for most legislative seats. In New York, where both parties run full legislative slates, not only are statewide candidates chosen by convention, but the stakes of statewide contests are so high that both parties have maximum incentive for running full slates.

In a state where a long-time minority party is trying to gain an equal footing, it must build up local party organizations enough to produce a complete, or nearly complete, legislative slate. In the 1920's the Democrats usually held only two or three seats in the Michigan legislature and contested no more than one-quarter of them; even in the 1930's, when they won occasional majorities in the legislature, they left as many as one-quarter of the seats uncontested.[17] At present virtually all seats are contested. In Maine the rejuvenated Democratic party has been contesting about four out of five legislative seats, compared to half in 1948.

California presents an example of the primary system carried to extremes at the expense of party organization. Until 1959 the state permitted cross filing in the primaries; candidates could file in the primaries of both parties, and until 1954 the primary ballot did not even indicate the party affiliation of candidates. As a consequence, the same candidate often won both primaries, particularly if he was the incumbent or for some other reason was well known. The Republicans benefited from this because they were the dominant party with more incumbents and because a party organization began to endorse certain candidates and discourage others from entering the primary. From 1922 through 1948, a single candidate won both primaries in two-thirds of the Senate elections and half the Assembly elections, with the proportions increasing in both houses.[18] Over two-thirds of these were Republican candidates. The development of Democratic Clubs to endorse candidates in the primary together with the modification and later abolition of cross filing paved the way for Democratic legislative victories in California.

Though it is usually the minority party in a state that fails to contest all legislative seats, there are examples of majority party failures too. In the New Hampshire House in 1950, 41 per cent of the seats were contested by both parties, 42 per cent had only Republican candidates, and 17 per cent had only Democrats. Duane Lockard has suggested that, in addition to the use of the direct primary, the large number of districts into which that state is divided (over 400) may increase the proportion that are politically lopsided.[19] During recent years in the Kentucky House, 40 per cent of the seats have been contested by both parties; the Democrats have won 47 per cent without opposition and the Republicans, 13 per cent. In that predominantly Democratic state there are pockets of Republican control in the southeastern mountains.

Within the states a variety of factors may determine which areas have strong enough party organizations to guarantee two-party contests. In general, the better the chances for party victory in a district, the more likely there is to be a candidate. To measure this accurately, it is necessary to analyze elections over a period of time. In Kentucky, there were 55 House districts (out of a total of 100) in which there was party competition in less than three out of six elections from 1947 through 1957; these are almost exclusively areas of traditional dominance by a single party. The most frequent two-party competition was found in districts where the two parties were closely balanced and in metropolitan centers, particularly in Jefferson County (Louisville), where both parties have strong organizations.[20]

Does this mean that two-party competition for legislative seats is most likely to be found in major urban areas? The urban party organizations are likely to have greater financial resources and more potential candidates than rural ones; the larger number of votes at stake for statewide offices may encourage the filing of a full slate. Nevertheless, there is no persistent pattern of greater competition in metropolitan areas. In Kentucky the Republicans, lacking deep roots in most rural areas, are particularly dependent on their growing suburban strength, and yet there are some metropolitan counties where they have not always run legislative candidates. In North Carolina, as in Kentucky, Republican strength in recent years has been greatest in the mountain areas and in the higher income sections of the

40

largest cities, but the Republicans have run a full legislative slate less often in these major cities than in many of the mountain and Piedmont counties. Since the Democrats contest virtually all legislative seats, the area of frequent or consistent two-party competition encompasses most of the western half of North Carolina, where the Republican party has had substantial strength for decades.

Though both parties in most states normally have substantial organization in the larger cities, the one-sided nature of some districts reduces two-party competition. Detroit, Milwaukee, and Boston are scattered examples of cities where the Republicans have not always run complete slates. In Maryland the Republican party, badly outnumbered in the legislature, has run nearly complete slates except in Baltimore City, where there have sometimes been considerable gaps in the lower income districts. Throughout the North the districts without Democratic candidates are primarily in rural areas while the districts uncontested by Republicans are found both in the heart of urban areas and in those rural areas dominated by Democrats.

If a party fails to run a legislative candidate only where it has little chance of winning, what difference does it make? The voters are deprived of a choice at the polls, but if they have been voting overwhelmingly for one party, this may appear to be only a theoretical limitation on their freedom. This failure of party organization becomes important primarily when the voters grow disillusioned with the party in power or are attracted by a new figure on the political scene and elect a governor from the minority party. That party is usually slow to provide candidates, at least able candidates, in all the legislative districts. A party that makes a serious bid for the governorship while running candidates for less than half the legislative seats, as

recently happened in both Kentucky and North Carolina, is insulting the intelligence of the voters. A party's
minority status in a district can become self-perpetuating
because there are few if any local candidates to preach
the party gospel to the voters. Though measurement
is impossible, there is no doubt that in some districts
a minority party deliberately avoids running candidates
for the legislature or other local offices as part of an
agreement with the majority party for patronage or
other favors. This is a temptation regularly confronting any party long out of power; when the minority suc-
cumbs, it is clearly depriving the voters of the right
to make a choice.

Competition in Legislative Primaries

In those legislative districts where only one party
often runs a candidate, does competition in the majority party primary provide a substitute for two-party
competition? On the surface, this would appear to be
true. V. O. Key's analysis has shown that primary
competition grows more likely as a party's chances of
winning increase; there is likely to be considerable
competition in sure districts, some contests in close
districts, and a distinct shortage of candidates in districts where the party's chances appear poor.[21] An analysis of Kentucky House districts shows that there is
much more likely to be primary competition in the
majority party in districts where the minority party
has seldom or never run a candidate in recent years.
In Kentucky districts, where the majority party is often
Democratic but sometimes Republican, the same pattern has prevailed for both parties except that, in the
districts that are safe for each party, the Republicans
have had somewhat more primary competition than
the Democrats have had.

42

The likelihood of winning a seat is not the only factor making primaries more or less frequent. We might expect that when an incumbent was seeking renomination there would be less competition in the primaries than when there was no incumbent. In some states this appears to be true, but in others incumbency appears to make little difference. In some states, such as Ohio and Wisconsin, primary contests are more frequent in urban than in rural areas, both in two-party districts and in those dominated by one party. V. O. Key has speculated that in many rural areas less effort and fewer resources are necessary to monopolize party position than in large urban centers characterized by a multiplicity of power centers. In a small rural district there may be relatively few persons interested in politics, making it easier for a small clique to maintain control.[22] This is not a universal pattern, however. In Kentucky, primary contests are just as frequent in rural as in urban districts. In a large number of the rural Kentucky districts the majority party is so dominant that it lacks the incentive to maintain organizational unity. In the closely competitive districts of the state, there is much *less* primary competition in some of the metropolitan areas where there are strong party organizations trying to unite the party behind a single slate of candidates.

In the frequent cases where legislative primaries take the place of two-party elections, the voters have a choice, but it may not be a meaningful choice. That is, the voters may have to choose between personalities, with little knowledge of what the candidates stand for. One of the greatest advantages of the two-party system is that it simplifies the voter's task. He is more likely to be aware of the general philosophy, viewpoint, and record of a party than to know much about an

43

individual candidate. In a state with an effectively functioning two-party system, there is considerable likelihood that legislators will support the stand of their party on major issues; this is a topic we shall explore more in the next chapter. When the voter's only choice comes in the primary, he is unlikely to perceive any clear differences between the candidates unless they are allied with well-recognized statewide factions. In a two-party state such factionalism is rare. It is more likely to be found in states dominated by one party, and these are the states where primaries most often replace elections as the significant or only contests. In many states where one party has some degree of domination, however, that party is splintered into a number of factions, which wax and wane with the political fortunes of particular candidates for statewide office. Politics in such states is most likely to be issueless, and the voter usually must choose candidates for both state and local office largely on the basis of personalities and promises.

In several states, both North and South, the dominant party has had persistent factions over a period of years. Examples are the Long and anti-Long factions in Louisiana, the Byrd machine and its opponents in Virginia, the Chandler and anti-Chandler groups in Kentucky, and the Proctor and anti-Proctor forces in Vermont. There is some likelihood that such factions will develop records and come to stand for something in the public mind, much as parties do. Though bifactionalism in a one-party state is a weak substitute for two-party politics, it offers the voter more rational choices than do a multiplicity of factions.

However meaningful these factions may be in state politics, they usually have little significance in legislative primaries. Duane Lockard has reported that "there is very little carryover of factional alignments into the legislature" in Vermont and New Hampshire, the two

New England states where he has found evidence of bifactionalism in the dominant Republican party.[23] In the Kentucky legislature there is sometimes evidence of the persistent statewide Democratic factionalism. In Kentucky legislative primaries, factionalism occasionally arises in the Democratic contests, most often in Jefferson County (Louisville), where the strong Democratic organization and its factional opponents often endorse separate slates. The best example of bifactionalism affecting legislative primaries is in Louisiana, where the Long faction developed a ticket system for both state and local contests. Many legislative candidates align themselves with a statewide faction publicly, while even more do so privately, according to Allan P. Sindler, who has studied Louisiana politics thoroughly. Public alignments have been particularly common in the southern part of the state; where the alignments are private or simply a matter of "common knowledge" it is difficult to tell how many of the voters are aware of them. The fact that legislative candidates may be aligned with a statewide faction, as in Kentucky or Louisiana, does not mean that most voters are conscious of this fact or that state issues play any significant role in the legislative primaries. Sindler concluded that more than half of the legislative primaries he studied in Louisiana were confined to local issues.[24]

When there is little or no competition in general elections, primaries are usually an inadequate substitute because the choice means less to the voter than the choice between Democratic and Republican candidates. Frequently there are no factions to take the place of truly competitive parties; where there are, these factions seldom extend to legislative primaries; where they do, the voters are unlikely to perceive that the factional candidates stand for significantly different policies.

Other Factors Creating Irresponsibility

We have shown that there are frequent gaps in party competition for legislative seats and many reasons why primary contests are a poor substitute. There are other factors decreasing the voter's range of choice or tending to make it meaningless. In some states a large proportion of the legislative districts are won repeatedly by one party or the other with lopsided margins. This may result from heavy concentrations of Democrats in urban centers and of Republicans elsewhere; it may result in part from the large number of small districts. Whatever the reason, there is often little party turnover in many districts, even in some two-party states. This situation may make the legislator insensitive to constituent opinion and may cause minority party candidates to carry out *pro forma* campaigns.

In a large majority of the states, between one-third and two-thirds of the legislators are serving their first terms. The high turnover rate in legislatures has frequently been noted and the resulting inexperience of most legislators is regularly deplored, but the political consequences of this are often overlooked. Since most of those who serve one or two terms are not defeated but retire voluntarily, the voter often loses his chance to pass judgment on the incumbent legislator at the polls. The voter must rely more on promises and less on records than would seem desirable. One cause of this high turnover is that in many multi-county districts the rotation principle is followed. The legislator's job is rotated evenly among the counties, so that no incumbent serves more than two or four years. Rotation may be based on tradition and practice or may result from a formal intra-party agreement in one or both parties. It not only causes turnover, but it may easily cause capable candidates to be passed over in favor of others from another county.

46

Elections and Party Responsibility

In the first chapter we defined party responsibility: the voter must know what the parties and the legislative candidates stand for, must be able to make a choice, and must be able to defeat those that have not fulfilled their promises. A survey of legislative elections reveals how seldom the voters have these choices in fact. The number of strictly one-party states is declining, but in those that remain (mostly southern) party responsibility is meaningless and factional responsibility is rare. In the remaining states, malapportionment sometimes makes it impossible for a majority (perhaps even a large majority) to choose the party it wants to control both the executive and legislative branches of government.

In choosing an individual legislator to represent him responsibly the voter often faces many obstacles. However competitive politics is in a state, many voters live in one-sided districts. If so, the voter may find that only one party runs a candidate, and that he has no vote unless he joins the majority party in order to make a choice in the primary among several candidates, all of whom repeat the same clichés or ignore issues entirely. If the voter is fortunate enough to have a choice between a Democrat and a Republican, he probably knows something about what the two parties in his state stand for. If the elected legislator does not vote with his party, ignores his campaign promises, or proves to be ineffective or corrupt, he may avoid punishment at the polls by not seeking re-election. If he does run, the voter may not learn enough from the campaign about the legislator's record to make an intelligent and informed judgment about him. It would seem that our model voter who benefits from responsible parties is a rarity.

THREE

VOTING ALIGNMENTS IN
THE LEGISLATURE

I always voted at my party's call,
And I never thought of thinking for myself at all.
                                        —H. M. S. PINAFORE

What role do political parties play in the decisions made
by state legislatures? Where parties are not important,
do factional or other alignments take their place? We
can answer these questions in two ways. In this chapter
we shall explore the evidence of party and factional
activity manifest in legislative roll calls. In the next
chapter we shall discuss the forms of party organization
that exist in various legislatures. Strong organization,
though one cause of party voting on roll calls, is not
likely to be found in states where other preconditions of
party voting do not exist.

We can start with the safe assumption that in a legislature where one party regularly has an overwhelming
majority the roll calls will produce no significant party
alignments. The handful of minority members may stick
together, but the large majority party is likely to be
divided because it represents such diverse groups and
because it has no incentive to maintain party unity.
We shall look for evidence of party voting primarily in
the stronger two-party states (categories C and D, and
possibly B. 2 in Tables 1a and 1b).

After we have eliminated the one-party states, however, we do not find a close correlation between the

intensity of two-party competition in state politics and the importance of party alignments in the legislature. A few years ago a committee of the American Political Science Association polled experts in the various states and concluded from their reports that party cohesion was strong in seventeen state legislatures, moderate in eleven, and weak in twenty (including the two nonpartisan legislatures). The seventeen where it was strong included roughly half of each of our categories B. 2, C, and D; the twenty where it was weak included all but one in category A, about half in categories B. 1 and B. 2, and a few others.[1] This and more detailed studies in specific states suggest that the closeness of party competition in the states is an important factor, but not the only one, causing disciplined party voting in the legislature.

The Measure of Party Voting

What do we mean by a high degree of party voting in the legislature? This is a relative matter. Compared to the British Parliament, with its highly disciplined parties and assured majorities for the government on all significant issues, few of the legislative bodies in this country—state or national—appear to have much party unity. It has often been fashionable to say that the parties in Congress have little meaning, that they resemble two empty bottles with different labels. In fact a number of studies have shown that party membership has much more influence than any other factor on voting in Congress. Party influence in state legislatures is often less than in Congress, but is sometimes equal or greater.

There are numerous ways of measuring and describing party voting, none of which is fully satisfactory for comparative purposes. In some states roll calls are taken on the final passage of most or all bills because of custom or constitutional requirements. In other states, as in Congress, roll calls are usually confined to the more important and more controversial issues, while in a few states they are held on only a few crucial issues. For comparative purposes it is desirable to eliminate unanimous and perhaps nearly unanimous roll calls from statistical compilations on party voting. We should recognize, however, that in some states most bills are unlikely to get a unanimous vote unless both party leaders have given their approval. An analysis of party voting limited to non-unanimous roll calls does provide an accurate measure of party *controversy*.

One test of party voting is the percentage of roll calls on which a majority of Democrats vote against a majority of Republicans; though a rough guide, this is a simple one for comparative purposes. Another frequently used tool of measurement is the index of cohesion, which shows how much unity a party has. If all the Democrats vote the same way, for example, the index would be 100; if they were equally divided for and against, the index would be 0; if three-quarters of them voted one way, the index would be 50. It is possible to measure the average index of cohesion for a party on roll calls, or how often the index of cohesion for a party is above a certain level. Perhaps the most useful technique is the measurement of "party votes": the roll calls on which the parties take opposite sides and each has a high index of cohesion, such as 80 or 60.

These techniques for measuring party voting have been applied to Congress by various writers. The compilations by the *Congressional Quarterly* show that the proportion of congressional roll calls on which the two parties have been opposed in recent years has ranged from 35 to 50 per cent.[2] On just over half of the foreign policy roll calls in the Senate from 1947 through 1958, the two parties took opposing stands. V. O. Key's figures show that for a sample of congressional sessions between 1933 and 1945 the Democrats had an average index of cohesion of 46 in the Senate and 59 in the House, while the Republican index was 52 in the Senate and 66 in the House.[3] Julius Turner applied the concept of a party vote (the two parties opposed, both with a cohesion index of at least 80) to the House for a sample of sessions from 1921 through 1948, and found that it varied from 7 to 31 per cent per session and averaged 17 per cent.[4] These findings provide some basis for comparison with the state legislatures.

Table 3 gives examples of party voting in a number of states studied by this writer and others, based on the frequency of roll calls on which the parties took opposite sides and the frequency of what we have called party votes.[5] Although there are some variations in the standards used by those studying the question, the table makes several conclusions evident. There is a wide range in the degree of party voting; party membership obviously means something very different in the Rhode Island and Missouri legislatures, for example. A second point, already mentioned, is that party voting does not vary proportionately with party competition in the state. The fact that in Rhode Island roll calls are few and are limited to major issues probably exaggerates the degree of party voting there. Nevertheless, it is significant that party discipline is highest in a state where the Democrats normally dominate the governorship and the House and the Republicans, the Senate. (Divided government in some states may have the effect of heightening party voting.) At the other extreme is Colorado, with a high degree of competition for control of all branches of government but with a relatively low level of party voting.

Most state legislatures deal with a much larger proportion of trivial and usually noncontroversial bills

TABLE 3

PARTY VOTING IN SELECTED STATE LEGISLATURES
ON NON-UNANIMOUS ROLL CALLS†

State	Total % Such Roll Calls		% When Each Party Has 80 Index of Cohesion		% When Each Party Has 60 Index of Cohesion		Years
	Senate	House	Senate	House	Senate	House	
Rhode Island	96	96			92	88	1931, '37, '51
Connecticut	90	83			71	77	1931-51
Massachusetts	82	87			36	56	1931, '37, '51*
New York	62	61	32	34			1947, '49*
Pennsylvania	64	81	52	56			1945*
Pennsylvania	34	43	22	30	25	35	1951
Ohio	52	40	15	7			1935, '49, '55, '57*
Illinois	53	54	15	17			1949*
Illinois					32	26	1949-57
New Hampshire	72	68			30	18	1931, '37, '51*
Washington	71	51	9	9			1945*
Kentucky	54	41	27	7			1944, '46*
Colorado	36	38	6	7			1941, '47*
Missouri	23	36	1	9			1945, '46*
California	20	32					1947, '49*
California	—	34	—	1			1957*
California	31	49	1	3			1959*

† All figures in this table are percentages of the total roll calls in a session with certain categories excluded from the total. In all states unanimous roll calls are excluded from the total. For those groups of legislative sessions marked with an asterisk, roll calls with 10 per cent or less of the members (or in some cases of both parties) voting in the minority are also excluded.

than Congress does, and often these require roll calls. Excluding the unanimous rolls calls (most of them on minor and local issues), the level of party voting is higher in several states than it is in Congress. Examples from Table 3 are New York, Pennsylvania, and the three southern New England states. Party voting approximates the congressional level in Ohio, Illinois,

New Hampshire, Washington, and (when the parties are closely competitive) in Kentucky; there is less party voting in Colorado, Missouri, and California. An average index of cohesion has seldom been calculated for each party in the state legislatures; where it has, the results bear out this comparison of various states with Congress.

The Causes of Party Voting

It is evident that in a number of states with varying degrees of two-party competition, party substantially influences voting in the legislature, while in others it has much less influence. What factors explain the differences?

Party voting is more evident in the larger, urban industrial states, where party alignments are most likely to follow urban-rural lines. Typically in such states the Democratic party has its greatest strength in one or a few metropolitan centers, particularly among labor groups, Catholic voters, racial and ethnic minorities, and persons with low incomes. The Republican voting strength comes from the higher-income suburbs, the rural towns, and at least some farm areas. Where one or two metropolitan centers are heavily Democratic, smaller cities are likely to be Republican; this is frequently true in New York, for example.

This urban-rural bipolarization of party strength is likely to be even more pronounced in the legislature. In the last chapter we explained how the district system in many states has maximized Democratic representation from urban centers and Republican representation from rural areas. In most of the heavily urban states included in Table 3, three-quarters or more of the Democratic legislators and only about one-third of the Republican legislators came from a few urban centers in each state. In states like these there is a clear difference between the constituencies of the two parties, and consequently there is often a clear difference in the parties' policies and legislative voting records.

In the most industrialized states the two parties draw their votes from the same groups that the national parties do in the North; they reflect the impact of the New Deal on national political alignments. In these states the issues that arise often resemble the domestic issues of national politics, and on these the state Democratic parties are generally liberal and the state Republican parties conservative. The two parties stand for something different, something more than contrasts in tradition and geography, and these differences are often reflected in legislative roll calls.

Massachusetts and New York are examples of such states. One writer says of Massachusetts:

> Legislators adapt to the surroundings, and the role of the party is such in Massachusetts that adaption to it is nearly mandatory. While it is true that there are many issues on which the position of the party is of no particular consequence, on the questions of first importance—the structure and operation of the government, matters involving labor law, public welfare, and economic regulation—the role of the party is often decisive.[6]

In a similar vein are these descriptions of New York, one written in 1948 and one in 1960:

> In each house in Albany there is a center aisle sharply dividing the legislative chamber. . . . The line is more than physically present. It is the line of party regularity, too. The leader of each house knows that at any time, by calling for a "party vote," his floor whip can furnish him enough support from his side of the aisle to pass any bill.[7]

The legislature of the state possesses a party discipline far superior to that found either in the United States Congress or in all but a few state capitals. Almost all major issues are determined by party-line votes; when dissenting votes are cast by party members, they are ordinarily cast by permission of the party leaders.[8]

In neither New York nor Massachusetts are the parties completely homogeneous, of course. There are often conflicts, particularly in the Republican party, between representatives from the major urban centers and those from smaller cities and towns, but these conflicts are likely to be resolved within each party prior to roll call votes.

Washington presents an example of a state where both parties are more heterogeneous and party unity is lower despite a high degree of organization in the legislative parties. A recent survey showed that, of the forty-six legislative districts existing from 1940 to 1958, thirty-three could be identified with varying degrees of certainty as Democratic or Republican. Thirteen of the twenty-one Democratic districts and five of the twelve Republican districts were in the three major urban counties, and many of the remainder in both parties were in rural areas. In other words, neither party is likely to be united by common interests. During the 1945 session referred to in Table 3, Democratic legislators were clearly divided into liberal and conservative wings, which roughly followed an urban-rural pattern.[9]

Although California is becoming heavily industrialized, its parties do not clearly follow an urban-rural pattern. The Senate apportionment system strengthens the rural wing of the Democratic party in the Senate and contributes to a lower level of party voting there than in the Assembly. A more basic factor discouraging party voting is the long tradition of nonpartisanship in

California politics. This has had a strong impact on the legislature, particularly on the Senate where party factors still have little effect on legislative organization. Until its weakening and eventual abolition in recent years, the cross-filing system also tended to blur party lines in the legislature because candidates seldom advertised their party affiliation and often won the nomination of both parties. The revitalization of the Democratic party, the election of that party's gubernatorial candidate in 1958, and the growth of Democratic Clubs that are issue-oriented and endorse candidates in the primaries are all factors restoring partisanship to the legislature. New legislators, in particular, appear to be more party-oriented. Yet, as Table 3 shows, these changes have so far brought about only a limited increase in party voting on roll calls.[10]

Typically in the states with lower levels of urbanization and industrialization the party alignment is least related to urban-rural lines. The Democrats may draw a substantial proportion of their support from rural areas either for traditional reasons or because of the national farm issue; there are few metropolitan centers, and even in these the Democrats may not consistently predominate. The apportionment system may give the Democratic legislative party a particularly strong rural character. Both parties usually have more diverse constituencies and consequently less unity on issues. The parties are less likely to have an ideological, programmatic base; it is hard to describe one as liberal and one as conservative. Legislators are likely to be elected more because of their personal ability and experience or because of voting traditions in the area than because of what their party stands for. In the more rural states fewer of the important issues concern labor, housing, social welfare, and the other problems common to the politics of urban states; when such issues arise they are less likely to cause party voting.

In most of the Plains states the minority Democratic parties made substantial gains in the late 1950's, though usually not enough to control the legislature. In states like Kansas, Iowa, and South Dakota the Democrats usually did particularly well in urban areas, but urban Democratic legislators were still outnumbered in most cases both by urban Republicans and rural Democrats. In other words, both parties remained primarily rural with urban wings, and there was little basis for difference between them.

A legislative party accustomed to minority status may develop considerable unity, despite the diverse constituencies of its members, when the party elects a governor and wins a majority or a large minority in the legislature. This proved to be true of the Democratic party in Kansas during the 1957 and 1959 sessions under a Democratic governor when the party's legislative membership was larger than usual—though still a minority. The Democrats voted with substantially greater unity than in previous sessions, presumably because for the first time in years a Democratic administration's program was at stake and because the Democratic membership had grown large enough to have some impact on legislation. In fact the increasing unity first became evident as Democratic membership increased in the session prior to the Democratic administration. Party voting in Kansas did not, however, reach the levels in the larger and more industrialized eastern states. A recent study of the 1957 session of the Wisconsin Assembly concluded that the Democratic party, still in minority then but growing in strength, had greater cohesion than the majority Republican party, which still controlled the governorship.[11]

Kentucky is another example of a state where both legislative parties are primarily rural; moreover, the Republican party usually controls no more than one-fourth of the legislative seats. Both of these factors tend to discourage party voting. There are few clear-cut differences between the parties, and individual Republican legislators follow the traditional behavior of members long in the minority by supporting parts of the Democratic administration's program in return for various kinds of favors. During the 1944 and 1946 sessions referred to in Table 3, however, the presence of a Republican in the governor's mansion and a larger minority representation than usual gave the party greater incentive for unity. During these two sessions party voting assumed importance in the Kentucky legislature, particularly on issues like the budget that involved the prestige of the Republican administration. The examples of these states suggest that in other states partisanship may be expected to flare up quickly in the legislature when a minority party gains an unusual degree of power.

Robert H. Salisbury has provided an excellent description of Missouri politics, which explains why party voting is low in the legislature of that state. There is not an urban-rural, or metropolitan-outstate party alignment. The Democrats draw about half their votes and the Republicans about 60 per cent of theirs from outside the St. Louis and Kansas City areas. Neither major city is highly industrialized or has militant labor unions. Moreover, "there are really no basic economic and social interests in conflict in the Missouri political arena," nothing comparable to the class conflicts familiar in more industrial states. "Exactly because the interest conflicts are minor, so the issues with which state government deals will be minor." Policy conflicts will be "local and specific," and the parties will develop little ideology. Salisbury aptly describes Missouri as a "politically bland state."[12]

One additional way of explaining why party voting occurs in some states more than others is to describe what types of issues cause party votes, with the two parties largely united in opposition to each other. Two major sources of such votes are welfare issues (health, education, and other services) and measures to regulate business and labor. In the more urban and industrialized states these are likely to be party issues as much as half of the time; on other roll calls at least one of the two parties is often united. In the rural states, however, there is not likely to be much unity in either party on these issues. In the urban states these issues are likely to be the best criteria for determining what difference there is between the parties, but in the more rural states it is often difficult to distinguish clearly between party stands.

Another type of issue that frequently causes party voting is one that involves the prestige and basic program of the state administration. The best examples are taxation and appropriations measures and appointments. In most of the states with considerable party voting these issues frequently produce party votes. Presumably a legislator usually tries to support the budget of a governor in his party, while the opposition may profit politically if it can force changes in the budget. Yet in some of the less industrial, more rural states there are seldom party votes in the legislature even on these issues. One reason is that both taxes and appropriations sometimes involve basic issues of social welfare and class interest on which both parties in these states may be split.

One type of issue that causes party voting in both urban and rural states is that involving the special interests of the parties. In William J. Keefe's words, "A large number of party conflicts develop on issues the primary concern of which is the party organization, not the public. The party, in this sense, is essentially a pressure group." The party may have an interest in a wide variety of bills, including local government, state administration, the civil service, registration and election laws, and legislative procedure. The party interest in the matter may not be evident on the surface. For example, the purpose of a bill to transfer a function from city to county control in a metropolitan center may be to give one party additional control over the function and perhaps additional jobs. Since most of these issues are of little interest to the voter, a record of high party unity in voting on them is hardly a measure of party responsibility. If in some states the relatively few roll calls with party votes deal largely with narrow party interests, the parties stand for even less in the voter's mind.[13]

Writers on state government frequently emphasize the urban-rural conflicts in the legislatures, and we have stressed the importance of an urban-rural party alignment in giving the parties a programmatic base. This suggests that there are significant urban-rural differences on most issues, or at least the most important issues, in state government. Actually there is a complex relationship between party and urban-rural factors, in which cause and effect can easily be confused. David Derge has made the most intensive efforts to clarify this relationship, in studies of Illinois and Missouri, states where neither legislative party is overwhelmingly urban or rural. Derge discovered that metropolitan legislators from both parties seldom voted together with a high degree of unity and there were very few cases in which most metropolitan legislators voted against most non-metropolitan legislators. In the roll calls of both legislatures party conflict was much more evident than a strictly urban-rural conflict. Thomas Flinn, using a much broader classification of urban counties, also found greater unity in each of the parties than in either the urban or rural delegation in the Ohio legislature.[14]

One reason for disunity among urban legislators may be that they represent voters with different interests. The metropolitan area includes both the slum tenements and the suburban homes with two-car garages. Moreover, if the urban category is stretched to include smaller cities, these may have interests competing with those of metropolitan centers. The Democrats often dominate in the central parts of cities and the Republicans in the suburbs. Derge found that Democratic and Republican legislators from the Chicago area often disagreed over bills designed to embarrass or place limitations on the Democratic-controlled government of Chicago. Substantive issues such as local taxation and annexation may be intertwined with maneuvering for partisan advantage. On measures applicable primarily to the metropolitan centers, Derge found that legislators from other areas tended to support the stand of their party colleagues in the urban centers or sometimes refused to support a measure that did not have bipartisan metropolitan support.

Divisions within urban delegations may apply not only to questions of city government but also to broader issues. Democratic urban legislators are likely to support expanded government expenses for unemployment compensation, housing, and a variety of welfare measures. Republican urban legislators are likely to represent the suburbs and smaller cities where constituents will have to pay for these measures but are less likely to benefit from them. There may be urban-rural differences overriding party considerations on some issues, but it is generally true to say that party considerations take precedence in the larger industrial states.

61

Part of the confusion about the importance of urban-rural differences arises from those states, like New York, Massachusetts, or Michigan, where the representation of metropolitan areas in the legislature is overwhelming Democratic and often the rest of the legislature is overwhelmingly Republican. This may result from the way district lines are drawn or the strength and weakness of various party organizations. The result is that the metropolitan centers may appear to speak with a single voice because some of the high-income, suburban areas may be swallowed up in larger districts and may lack a Republican spokesman. Likewise what looks like the unity of non-metropolitan legislators may be fundamentally the unity of Republican legislators. Moreover, in these states where each party represents a rather homogeneous group of voters, conflicts between the two groups over issues may be intensified.

Other Patterns of Voting

In the absence of strong party voting, what other factors are likely to determine the pattern of roll calls in the legislature? In fact there is no complete substitute for party voting. Normally there are no other blocs of legislators that vote together with as much unity as we have seen Republicans and Democrats doing in some states. What we find in examining the states with low party voting is that during certain periods of time or on certain types of issues there are likely to be alignments along factional, urban-rural, or regional lines. Factional alignments will vary in importance from session to session, while urban-rural and regional alignments usually become evident only on a limited number of legislative issues.

Factionalism is most frequent in those states where a single party has a consistent majority or has complete control. Two persistent factions are likely to be found in the dominant party if they represent two distinct interests or regions in the state. Sometimes a political leader, such as Huey Long in Louisiana or Herman Talmadge in Georgia, makes such an impact on the politics of his state that his supporters and opponents form two factions that last for many years. In other states the single dominant party is characterized by multi-factionalism: candidates for major state office form their own coalitions, which are soon replaced as new candidates appear on the political scene. However strong a governor may be while in office, he usually has little influence on the choice of a successor in such states; there is little or no continuity in the factions.

Any strong governor in the dominant party may be able to win temporary support from a majority of legislators for the bulk of his program. He has no certainty of such support, however, and must usually gain it in large part through job patronage, highway projects, and other such lures. In a state with continuing bifactionalism in the dominant party there is the possibility of greater continuity in legislative bloc-voting. We should not attach too much importance to this factional voting. In the previous chapter we pointed out that statewide factional alignments are seldom reflected in legislative primaries. Two factions in the legislature *may* come to stand for different interests and policies, much as parties do in *some* of the two-party states, but often they are rooted only in personalities and patronage.

On the basis of questionnaires sent to experts in the various states, a committee of the American Political Science Association in 1954 concluded that factionalism was strong in several of the states where one party had a dominant position (Kentucky, New Mexico, New Hampshire, Wisconsin) and that there was a bifactional pattern in half of the states which it defined as one-party (Arizona, Arkansas, Georgia, Kansas, Louisiana, North Dakota, Oklahoma, Tennessee, Virginia).[15] One example it cited was North Dakota, where the Republican party was sharply divided into conservative and progressive wings. In another Republican-dominated state, Vermont, Duane Lockard has concluded that factional alignment in the legislature becomes apparent only when there has been a sharp cleavage in the gubernatorial primary or when a governor sponsors an aggressive legislative program. "From time to time factional alignments do arise, but the usual situation is more fluid and unstructured. Groups appear to form, disperse, and reform with ever-changing composition depending upon the question before the house." [16]

Bifactionalism is more prevalent in Louisiana than in most southern states. During Huey Long's reign and during some of the subsequent administrations, Louisiana legislators could be clearly identified as either for or against the governor on a number of the controversial issues that arose. Kentucky is a state where bifactionalism in the majority Democratic party seldom extends to legislative issues; the governor normally has widespread support in the legislature at least during the first biennial session of his term. In 1958, during the second session of Governor A. B. Chandler's term, however, the legislators were sharply split into Chandler and anti-Chandler groups on a number of important roll calls, and the governor had to rely on Republican votes for his victories. In Virginia the organization of Senator Harry Byrd has long dominated the Democratic party, while the opposition has not been strong enough to justify the description of the state as bifactional. From time to time Democratic legislators from urban and northern Virginia areas have voted as a bloc in opposition to the Byrd machine. Somewhat similarly, the dominant faction of the Democratic party in Georgia has drawn its support largely from rural areas, and the urban legislators, handicapped by the apportionment system, have seldom been able to challenge the administration in the legislature.

Factionalism in the legislatures of one-party states is a subject that deserves more study, particularly because the facts constantly change. In a number of states factional alignments in the dominant party are reflected from time to time in the legislative roll calls. These alignments are seldom of long standing and usually appear only on scattered issues. Persistent factionalism is less evident on roll calls than in the county-by-county primary voting statistics. We must conclude that in the legislature factions are usually pale shadows of parties.

Where there is no partisan or factional pattern in legislative voting we look for urban-rural and regional differences. Potentially the sharpest urban-rural conflicts are in the major industrial states, where we have already seen that a strong two-party system is the rule and party voting is frequently present. Elsewhere it is always possible that an urban-rural split will develop on particular issues, but there is no such dominant pattern in the voting. Urban and rural legislators are most likely to differ over the allocation of state funds for highways, education, and other purposes. There may be different views on daylight saving time or on such "moral" questions as liquor laws and pari-mutuel betting. Urban legislators may have difficulty winning rural support for municipal legislation on such questions as annexation, planning and zoning, and home rule. In the South, rural legislators, particularly from black-belt counties, may vote differently on racial questions and school desegregation than do urban representatives. Some issues divide a state along regional lines; an example is the prolonged controversy over water resources between northern and southern California.

It is not difficult to find examples of issues on which urban and rural legislators have differed. There is no doubt that in some states the distribution of state grants to local governments has been based on formulae designed by rural-dominated legislatures to favor rural counties. Important though some of these issues are, they usually make up a relatively small proportion of the legislature's business, and consequently the urban-rural alignment does not dominate voting in the legislature.

Where party and faction do not often determine legislative voting, there is not likely to be any single pattern. Instead the careful observer may find shifting coalitions representing at times factions, regions, urban-rural differences, or liberal and conservative philosophies. One writer on Arizona believes that the principal cleavage in that legislature is a conservative-liberal one. The conservatives include farmers and ranchers, mining groups, and both urban and rural business interests. The weaker liberal group draws primarily urban support. Republican legislators generally vote with the conservative Democrats, and the liberal and conservative blocs are relatively cohesive in the legislature.[17] In Florida, where Democratic gubernatorial factions are transitory, the legislature is run by a coalition of men, linked by personal ties, and representing rural, conservative, and segregationist views.[18] Texas has been described as a state where "temporary combinations on particular issues" result from sectional, liberal-conservative, rural-urban, and pro- or anti-administration alignments.[19]

In a thorough study of the Alabama House, Murray Havens found that urban-rural conflict was present to a significant degree on just over one-fourth of the roll calls, including a large number dealing with reapportionment. Often there was no significant conflict where it might be anticipated, such as on municipal or farm legislation. Since urban interests were in a minority, they often sought alliances with rural legislators from the northern part of the state or those allied with the state administration. On some issues the representatives in one or another region displayed considerable unity; on others there was a sharp contrast between the voting of supporters and opponents of the administration, although one-fourth of the legislators could not be put in either category.[20] The legislature was characterized by overlapping groups whose relative importance varied on the different roll calls. Roll call statistics may exaggerate the cohesion of legislative groups on occasions when their members are simply responding to the same pressure groups. The Alabama study, for example, showed that urban legislators supported measures for the licensing of barbers on which others were divided. This is not an important urban-rural issue, but presumably urban barbers were better organized in favor of the measure.

It is difficult, and in fact misleading, to define some clear pattern in most of the states where there is little party voting. The factional voting created by political events in one session may vanish in the next; coalitions of interests shift from issue to issue. These various coalitions lack the tradition and habit of unity as well as the common interests that hold a party together in the legislative voting of some states. Our evidence suggests that there are relatively few roll calls on which the interests of a region or of urban or rural areas are so obvious that the legislator must vote a certain way.

Constituents and Pressure Groups

The frequency with which an individual legislator votes with his party depends not only on the type of party system or the degree of industrialization in the state but also on his relationship to his constituency. Party voting is more likely in states where each party represents relatively homogeneous groups. When there is such a clear difference between Democrats and Republicans, a legislator is more likely to vote with his party if his district is typical of most others represented by his party. In the typical two-party states of the industrial North, the Democratic legislator from an urban working-class district and the Republican from a small town are likely to vote loyally with their respective parties. Among the Democrats elected from small towns or prosperous suburbs and the Republicans representing working-class districts will be found most of the legislative mavericks. When members of this latter group see a conflict between party and constituency, their vote is not predictable; it may go either way. One factor determining how such cross-pressured legislators vote is the closeness of their recent electoral margins. Since their districts are often not typical of most others in the party, their re-election is often in doubt. The greater the doubt, and the closer their last victory, the more likely they are to ignore the party leaders if they believe the demands of their constituents require it.

This pattern of legislative behavior seems logical in theory; it has also been proven in practice by studies of the lower house in Massachusetts, Pennsylvania, and Wisconsin. We know from these studies that legislators from atypical and especially from close districts are more independent of party in their voting. They are usually conscious of their insecurity and the conflicts between the demands of their party and their constituents. Sometimes their plight is clear enough so that the party leadership is quite tolerant when these members vote against the party, at least on certain issues. The study in Pennsylvania indicated that the voting of state senators does not vary so much with the types of districts.

The larger, more varied districts and the four-year terms of senators in that state are possible explanations for this difference.[21]

One reason for the high party voting in the legislatures of some northern industrial states is that many legislators are regularly elected by lopsided margins or sometimes without opposition. Theoretically in a state where a significant proportion of legislators are elected without a contest, party discipline should be particularly high, but in most such states one party has such large and consistent legislative majorities that there is little incentive for party unity.

In describing the conflicting pressures of party and constituency that a legislator sometimes faces, we must remember that on many issues he is likely to find that his constituents have neither a clear interest nor any opinion. Constituency interests may be most apparent on broad social and economic issues, on questions of taxation, and on narrower issues affecting some group that is well organized in a particular district.

As he reads his mail and answers his phone, the legislator becomes acutely aware of the organized groups in his district. He learns that individual constituents seldom contact him except at the behest of an organization. He may conclude that the average voter knows and cares nothing about what he does. As soon as he wins election, the legislator is likely to receive letters from state and local organizations, congratulating him, offering assistance, and summarizing the legislative interests of the group. There may be questionnaires asking his views on a variety of issues or seeking a commitment to some proposal. Since most mail results from organized groups, the legislator may receive more on a highly specialized topic than on a major issue of broad public interest. The legislature is an arena for competing economic interests, all of which hope to make the state their ally in the free enterprise system. Representatives of horse-racing interests write that the introduction of dog racing to Kentucky would damage not *only* them but the state's way of life. The chiropractors are upset by a bill sponsored by the state's medical association. Bank presidents wire to protest a bill that would permit small loan companies to loan larger amounts. Florists and nurserymen want licensing laws to limit competition. Local dairies want legislation to guarantee "orderly marketing practices" and undercut the methods used by chain stores. These examples from the mail of a single member during one session simply illustrate the range of competing economic pressures to which the legislator is subjected.

The legislator encounters a wide variety of pressure groups during his term of office. The letters just cited provide examples of specialized economic groups. Though such a group may have relatively few members in a single district, it may be important because of its members' influence or the intensity of its lobbying efforts. Another category of pressure groups is the major labor, business, and farm organizations (the AFL-CIO, the Chamber of Commerce, and the Farm Bureau, for example). Unlike the specialized economic groups, these organizations tend to take stands on a wide variety of issues, and because of their prestige and broad membership base their views are usually listened to with respect in the legislature. In certain states one or another of these groups may play almost a dominant role in the legislature, gaining many of its requests and holding a virtual veto over legislation it opposes. Examples would be the role of the Farm Bureau in Vermont and the labor unions in Rhode Island and West Virginia. Nor is economics the only motivation for pressure groups. A church group, the League of Women Voters, or the Parent-Teachers Association, for example, can influence the legislature if it demonstrates that a significant number of its members are knowledgeable about and intensely interested in some topic. The influence of women in lobbying activities should not be underrated; they frequently have not only intense concern about problems but more time to devote to politics than do their husbands.

Another type of organized pressure comes from governmental agencies and personnel. School teachers are usually well-organized, intelligent and persistent in presenting their demands, and politically important because they are numerous in every district and because the public is concerned about educational problems. City and county officials in a legislator's district get attention not only because they may be politically powerful but also because the legislator respects their knowledge of local affairs and is trying to serve the needs of local governmental units in his district. Leading officials in state agencies, who often campaign for specific bills, carry weight because of their expert knowledge and because they may be able to provide services for the legislator.

More than half of the states require all lobbyists to register, and about two-thirds of this number require periodic reports on receipts and expenditures. The lobbying registration laws are seldom strictly enforced, but they do provide the legislator with some minimum information about the persons who are trying to influence his views. They also provide us with some insight into the scope of lobbying. In 1957 the number of registered lobbyists ranged from 23 in South Carolina and 71 in Rhode Island to 587 in Florida and 779 in Nebraska. Reports of expenditures, which are probably often incomplete, are frequently over $100,000 and sometimes as much as $300,000.[22]

A number of registered lobbyists are simply the un-

71

paid officers of various groups, who may appear at the state capital a few times during the session to lobby for specific measures. Some of the largest organizations, on the other hand, have a headquarters staff of several persons who devote most of their time to lobbying during the legislative session. In addition, there are the professional lobbyists, usually lawyers and often ex-legislators, who sell their services to a variety of smaller groups that cannot afford a full-time representative.

The men who devote all or most of their time to lobbying are usually skilled and experienced in the legislative process. Lobbying, like any other business these days, has become a skilled profession. It is no longer a matter of plying legislators with food and drink and handing them a large-denomination bill at the end of the evening. Today's lobbyist must understand the intricacies of the legislative process, and he must know the men with whom he deals. He must understand who exercises power, who is most influential on specific types of measures, which members are amenable to which types of pressure or persuasion.

The skillful lobbyist can do many favors for a legislator. He can provide information, assistance in drafting bills, perhaps even help in passing one of the legislator's own bills. The legislator who has no staff and perhaps lacks experience at the capitol may appreciate these services. Lobbyists sometimes imply that they have more to offer: clients for the legislator-lawyer, customers for the legislator-businessman, or campaign support for the legislator who wants re-election. The fundamental task of the lobbyist is to persuade the legislator that he represents many constituents who are deeply concerned about the passage or defeat of a bill. To accomplish this, the lobbyist from time to time must try to persuade a substantial number of his group to write to their legislators. Though this is a powerful weapon, it is usually held in reserve, because a mass of identical letters are worth little and it is difficult to evoke many independent letters from constituents.

Perhaps the most useful tool for understanding the role of the pressure group in the legislative process is David Truman's concept of *access*. Truman points out that "access to the legislature is of crucial importance at one time or another to virtually all such groups. . . . In some forms it provides little more than a chance to be heard; in others it practically assures favorable action. Some groups achieve highly effective access almost automatically, whereas it is denied to others in spite of their most vigorous efforts." [23] In the legislative process of most states there are a considerable number of access points. The skilled lobbyist will know which point of access is most valuable and perhaps most vulnerable—the speaker, the committee chairman, the governor's assistant. In states where the party organization is strong, the lobbyists are likely to concentrate attention on the party leaders. Under these circumstances, the individual legislator may not even be conscious of pressure group activities on some important issues. In some states major pressure groups have developed close alliances with one or the other party. Examples of this are the ties between labor groups and the Democratic party and between business groups and the Republican party. On other occasions a pressure group may win party cooperation by the promise of help at the polls or aid in winning the passage of party bills.

Where party authority is weaker or where a group lacks access to party leadership, the lobbyist needs access to the individual legislator. It is not enough to be able to talk with him; the lobbyist must establish rapport with the legislator. This is one reason the ex-legislator makes a good lobbyist; he has personal access to most of the members. Most pressure groups can

73

count on the active cooperation of at least one or a few current members of the legislature. In any legislature there is likely to be a present or past official of a county farm bureau, a labor union official, a doctor, a state or local official of the Chamber of Commerce. In addition there are members who are eager to cooperate with these groups because of personal sympathies or the affiliations of their constituents. Such legislators are usually willing to work actively for the objectives of the group. They will introduce bills, cooperate in tactical planning, and keep the lobbyist informed about legislative developments and rumors. Such members are often strategically placed on the committees dealing with the bills of interest to the group. Above all, they provide the lobbyist with informal access to other members of the legislature. The legislature is a "club," and the lobbyist who is invited in as member or guest is far more likely to be able to influence its decisions than the one who is left on the outside.

We have been examining the question of access from the viewpoint of the lobbyist. Recent research has shown that legislators vary widely in their perceptions of lobbyists. Some of them, particularly newcomers, profess to be ignorant of lobbies and lobbyists that are well known to other members, others are critical of pressure groups and deny that they have a legitimate role in the legislative process, and still others are firmly committed to the views of certain groups and suspicious of the activities of other groups. The variety of attitudes and the depth of suspicion shared by some members indicate the importance to the lobbyist of achieving access through intermediaries whom the legislator does trust.[24]

A mere description of the number of lobbyists and the techniques they employ tends to exaggerate the pressure put on any individual member. In fact there are a number of mitigating circumstances, as we have seen. The legislator is sympathetic to and even in alliance with some groups. Sometimes the efforts of the lobbyists are concentrated on party leaders. Some groups, however noisy, may be ignored because they are insignificant in the member's district. Some of the demands of groups may be acceded to because they do not conflict with the vital interests of the party or of his district. Finally, a number of legislators are relatively secure in their districts and can afford to ignore the demands of most groups; they may yield to persuasion, but they are not under pressure.

Pattern and Variety in Legislative Voting

Of the many contrasts among state legislatures, perhaps the greatest are in the patterns of roll call voting. In a few states party affiliation is the key to voting behavior on most issues. In a number of states party alignments, though evident on only a fraction of the roll calls, appear to be the most significant factors. On the other hand, in some states party alignments are seldom or never significant in the voting. Party voting is most likely in states where each of the parties is relatively homogeneous and policy-oriented, where there is a political bipolarization along urban-rural lines. This tends to occur in the more industrial states. It may also be significant, at least temporarily, where the second party is rebuilding and challenging the majority party. In two-party states where the parties do not stand for anything, the parties are likely to vote as blocs only on issues affecting their narrow interests. If there is no pattern of party voting, a wide variety of factional, regional, or urban-rural patterns may appear. These are unlikely to last long or to encompass many issues; they appear and disappear with changing issues, circumstances, and personalities on the political scene. Without party voting, there is little pattern to the roll calls.

The absence of party pressure does not necessarily give the legislator more independence; it may simply make him more susceptible to interest groups. Where the party is strong, these groups are not inactive but direct their efforts more to the party leadership. Where the party is weak, interest groups are likely to have more influence and to exert more pressure on the individual legislator.[25] The effectiveness of a particular lobbyist depends a great deal on his success in achieving access to those members of the legislature most likely to control the fate of his bills. Strong political parties can moderate and balance the demands of competing interests more successfully than can a single legislator. It is possible, of course, that agreement between the leaders of a party and a pressure group can make the whole party serve the interests of the group, and in some states certain groups have formed close alliances with either the Democratic or Republican party. The party is more likely than the individual legislator to recognize the need of balancing group demands, however, and its failure to do so is more obvious to the voter.

The factors that determine legislative voting vary not only from state to state but among individual members of the legislature. The legislator is sensitive to the views of his constituents, even when he is unsure of these views, and his sensitivity is greatest if his recent electoral margins have been narrow. In states where party ties are strong, he may accede to the demands of party leaders unless they clearly conflict with constituent interests. He may respond to the appeals of pressure groups, or even work closely with them, if they are strong in his district or if his own background makes him sympathetic to them. The less party unity there is in a state legislature, the greater the variety of other factors that may influence a member.

FOUR

POLITICAL ORGANIZATION OF
THE LEGISLATURE

Things are seldom what they seem,
Skim milk masquerades as cream.
　　　　　—H. M. S. PINAFORE

Nowhere do the realities of the legislative process differ more from the formal, legal framework than in the organizational structure. On paper, the various legislatures seem to be carbon copies of Congress, each with its hierarchy of elected leaders, committees, and sometimes caucuses. In practice these leaders and institutions differ widely in their power and operating techniques. Once more we must distinguish among legislatures with varying degrees of party competition. Where there are two strong parties we may expect, but not always find, well-organized party leadership. Where parties are weak, the organizational structure sometimes reflects the dominance of certain factions or regions.

The Leaders

The role of the presiding officer is often different in the House and Senate. The Speaker of the lower house is clearly the most powerful figure in that branch; he is elected by the membership and represents whatever party or faction has a majority. All but eleven of the states have a lieutenant governor, and, except in Hawaii and Massachusetts, that official presides over the upper house of the legislature (and in Nebraska over the

77

unicameral body).[1] In the thirteen states where the members of the Senate elect their own presiding officer, he usually has powers comparable to those of the Speaker of the House. Where the lieutenant governor presides, he frequently must share power with an elected president pro tem or with a committee of Senate leaders. Not only is he a member of the executive branch, but he may represent a party or faction different from that of a majority in the Senate. In the states where divided government often exists, the lieutenant governor is most unlikely to be given powers as broad as those of the Speaker of the House.[2]

In two-party states the Speaker of the House and the elected presiding officer in the Senate are in fact chosen by the majority party caucus as its first order of business at the start of the session. Though the minority party nominates its own candidates for these posts, this is one issue on which party lines traditionally hold firm and the majority party's candidate is chosen. Party lines can be broken, however, even in states where the parties are strongly organized. In 1959 the Illinois Democrats held a five-vote majority in the House, their first since 1949, but there was a sharp division between Chicago and downstate Democrats. The Republican governor took advantage of this split and supplied the votes to elect a downstate Democrat, who had been outvoted by Chicago representatives in the Democratic caucus. In states where party lines are usually weak, the choice of the majority caucus may not always become Speaker. In California, for example, members of the minority party have sometimes held the balance of power in a contest between two members of the majority party for the speakership, while in the Senate, party affiliation has had little to do with the election of a president pro tem.[3] Where party is weak there is sometimes factional competition for the leadership posts, as in Kentucky.

78

In Florida a bloc of rural legislators has been able to hold the leadership positions during most recent sessions of the legislature.

Contests for the top legislative posts sometimes start long before the session begins and involve skillful bargaining for votes. An extreme example is Florida, where the campaigns often start four years early and the choice is actually made early in the session preceding that in which the presiding officer will serve. This pattern of election in Florida helps to preserve control by a rural bloc and minimizes the governor's influence on the selection.[4] In California the campaign for the Assembly speakership usually lasts several months. Wherever there is intensive campaigning, the promise of choice committee assignments seems to be the most important bargaining weapon in the hands of candidates. The governor often has a decisive voice in the choice of elected legislative leaders, but this is not consistently true even in states with a strong governor. During the 1961 session of the California legislature a powerful Democratic leader won signed pledges of support from a majority of members in the Assembly in his campaign for the speakership, confronting the Democratic governor with a virtual *fait accompli*.[5] In New York a Republican candidate for Speaker in 1959 had at least the passive support of the Republican governor, but he was not assured of election until he had satisfied the demands of a bloc of upstate Republican legislators, who were reluctant to approve a Speaker from the metropolitan area.[6]

In a few states legislative leaders hold their positions with a tenacity that rivals the late Sam Rayburn's. For example, in the lower house in Rhode Island, the Speaker and Democratic floor leader have held those posts continuously since 1941. Rotation in office is more common, sometimes but not always because the leaders seek higher political office or retire from politics. In Florida the few key posts are rotated among a handful of legislators in the inner circle of rural leadership. In Illinois, when a party regains control of the legislature after a period in the minority, it is likely to bypass former leaders who are still members; in Kentucky this often occurs when a Democratic faction regains control.

The choice of leaders is important because many of them have extensive control over the organization and functioning of the legislature and particularly the appointment of committees. The Speaker of the House is given the authority to choose members of the standing committees, and usually their chairmen, in all of the states except Alaska and Kentucky; in only two other states is his choice subject to approval by the House or a committee on committees. Senate practice varies widely; committees are appointed in fifteen states by the lieutenant governor, in six by the president pro tem, in twelve by the president of the Senate, in twelve by a committee (sometimes with Senate confirmation), and in five by the Senate itself.[7] In both houses members of special and conference committees usually are chosen by the presiding officer.

In some states political controversy has raged over the appointment power. In Kentucky, for example, when a Republican became lieutenant governor in 1944 the authority was taken away from him and given to Democratic leaders in the Senate; appointment by committee continued thereafter except during the four years of the Chandler administration. In Kansas the power to appoint committees and to preside over working sessions of the Senate has regularly been taken away from lieutenant governors who were either Democrats or members of a dissident Republican faction.[8] In 1951 there was a prolonged effort in the California Assembly to strip the Speaker of several powers, including the appointment of committees and the assignment of bills to them. The issue was not a partisan one, but a rank-and-file effort to limit the Speaker's authority. One argument used by the rebels was that lobbyists had too great an influence over the Speaker's choice of committee members. The legislators eventually adopted a compromise that did not affect these powers of the Speaker.[9]

The authority provided by the rules to the Speaker or to a presiding officer in the Senate may not in fact be exercised exclusively by that individual. The choice of majority members may be shared, as in the state of Washington, by a committee on committees, or it may be influenced in some states by the governor. In states with a strong two-party system the choice of minority members is normally delegated to the minority leadership. This, for example, is true in Illinois, where the views of the minority leaders on committee assignments are always respected.

In most states the legislative leaders who choose committee members have much greater authority than is true in Congress. Seniority is likely to have some influence over the choice, but it is much less important than in Congress, largely because there are seldom many legislators with more than a few years of seniority. The leaders usually try to preserve a party balance roughly proportionate to that in the legislature and often try to maintain some geographic balance. Despite these restrictions, the legislative leader—particularly the Speaker of the House—usually has vast opportunities to determine the fate of legislation through his choice of committees. He may be under considerable pressure from organized groups to pack certain committees with members sympathetic to those interests. A strong presiding officer, perhaps representing the interests of the governor, will place on certain key committees men who can be depended on to support the party, faction, or interests to which the presiding officer belongs.[10]

Perhaps the greatest contrast with congressional practice is that when a new session begins the presiding officer can and sometimes does remove a legislator from a choice committee to discipline him for a disloyal voting record. Though there may be few examples of such discipline, the existence of this power makes its frequent exercise unnecessary in some states. Where factions are important in the dominant party, factional loyalty is likely to be a prerequisite for choice committee assignments.

The importance of leadership control over committee assignments is magnified by the fact that the Speaker in forty-five states and the presiding officer of the Senate in forty-two states assign bills to committee, and in many cases these officers can assign bills arbitrarily, unbound by jurisdictional rules. In other states a committee usually has this function.[11]

The 1946 Legislative Reorganization Act specified the jurisdiction of congressional committees so precisely that the leadership in Congress has little if any chance to steer bills to favorable committees. Many state legislatures, however, operate with a number of committees having broadly descriptive titles, such as Judiciary, Ways and Means, Executive and Legislative Affairs, or Kentucky Statutes, for example. These are likely to be committees on which the legislative leadership has placed men that it can trust. The leadership will then refer to these committees both the important bills that it desires to see promptly passed and the dangerous bills it wishes to kill. Even where jurisdictional niceties are not so blatantly ignored, the legislative leadership is likely to exercise some discretion in the assignment of important bills.

In addition to the formal control over the appointment of committees and the assignment of bills to them, the Speaker in some states exercises considerable power in presiding over the House. This is an area where an examination of legislative rules provides little information; only first-hand observation of ever-changing practice would show how much power the Speaker exercises from the chair. A number of years ago one writer observed that:

> . . . it is a common practice for state presiding officers to use their powers of recognition and the entertainment of parliamentary motions and the declaring of the result of votes, in an extremely arbitrary manner. Indeed, it is correct to say that, in many cases, the state legislative chambers are "bossed" rather than provided with the benefit of responsible leadership.[12]

The presiding officer of a state legislature has greater opportunity for arbitrary action than would be possible in Congress because his actions are less publicized, because his party or faction often has complete dominance, and because rank-and-file members are usually ignorant of the rules. Thus the Speaker on occasion may recognize some members and ignore others, cut off debate or extend it, ignore demands for a roll call, or exercise wide discretion in judging voice votes. Even when a mechanical voting device is used, the Speaker may determine when the machine is to be closed and the votes counted; he can leave the machine open while votes are changed and absentees rounded up, or he can record the vote quickly either to pass or kill a bill. Control by the Speaker may be sophisticated or crude; it ranges from the skillful use of the parliamentary tactics to blatant attacks of legislative deafness or blindness. By and large it is true to say that the presiding officer in the Senate is unlikely to exercise such wide discretion in the chair unless he has been elected by the Senate membership.

In addition to the presiding officers, in most states there are floor leaders for the various parties or factions. According to a survey taken a few years ago about thirty state legislatures regularly had floor leaders and a few others had them occasionally.[13] In a two-party state the majority and minority floor leaders play roles similar to their counterparts in Congress. The majority leader often assists the presiding officer in planning committee assignments and developing legislative strategy; on the floor he manages the administration's bills. In a tightly run legislature a typical scene on the floor during the closing days of the session may resemble a dialogue between the Speaker and majority leader with a chorus of "ayes" in the background. The minority leader, of course, acts as spokesman and strategist for his party. While the floor leaders are often chosen along with the candidate for Speaker or president pro tem at a caucus of the party, the governor normally tries to exercise some influence over his party's choices, and in some states the Speaker picks the majority leader.

A floor leader is often found also in a legislature dominated by a single party, where he is not likely to be elected but rather designated, formally or informally, by the governor. In Alabama, for example, the governor has regularly designated a leader in each house since 1927. There he works in close cooperation with the governor and the Speaker or lieutenant governor. He can get immediate recognition from the presiding officer in order to change the trend of debate or make motions to table an objectionable amendment or to vote on a pending measure.[14] The governor's floor leader in a one-party state, in short, plays much the same role as a majority leader in a two-party state. The greatest difference is that usually there is no opposition leader unless a well-organized anti-administration faction exists.

Leadership . Committees

Most state legislatures have one or more committees, usually composed of the leadership, that play an important role in directing the business of the legislature. They may be labeled rules, policy, or steering committees or the committee on committees. They serve a variety of functions, the nature of which is not always clearly indicated by the title of the committee. Some are bipartisan bodies, while others contain only majority party members. In some states a single committee serves most of the functions, while in others the functions are divided among several. It is impossible to outline any "typical" pattern of functions and titles for such committees, but we can describe the various things these committees often do.

We have already pointed out that the appointment of standing committees is the function of a committee in a dozen Senates and in a very few lower houses. Such committees are usually bipartisan; they frequently have the title of Committee on Committees and serve that function primarily, but in a few states this duty is handled by a committee with broader powers. In a few states a committee has the power to refer bills to committees. An interesting example is the Reference Committee of the Ohio House, which also has the authority to screen out frivolous or duplicate bills.

Legislatures often have rules committees, usually chaired in the House by the Speaker. Other legislative leaders often serve on these committees in both branches. As a minimum such a committee normally is responsible for recommending changes in the rules under which the legislative body operates. Though potentially significant, this power alone does not give the committee day-to-day importance. In some states, such as California, the rules committee has administrative functions, controlling patronage, approving legislative expenditures, and screening resolutions to establish interim committees. In most state legislatures the rules committee does not have the power to determine priorities of bills as does the Rules Committee of the U. S. House of Representatives. Legislation is usually brought to the floor according to the order in which it is reported by the various committees.[15]

In several states, however, the rules committee does have the power to determine priorities and to select those bills that will reach the floor of the legislature. Usually the rules do not permit the committee to assume such authority until the closing days or weeks of the legislative session, when most important bills are usually passed. Legislative leaders have been known to stall legislative action, to adjourn sessions after a few minutes, in order to prevent passage of objectionable bills a few days before the Rules Committee is to assume its control over legislation.

In those states where the rules committee controls which bills reach the floor late in the session, it is often a powerful committee and a major tool of majority control. Though the minority party or faction may be included on it, the rules committee is normally under the firm control of the majority leadership. Alabama provides a good example of powerful rules committees in both houses, which, like their counterpart in the U. S. House, use special orders to advance bills to prompt floor action. In the closing days of the session, the committees meet daily to consider requests for special orders. By that time the legislative calendar is so crowded that bills are most unlikely to pass without such priority treatment. Likewise in Florida the rules committees determine the order for considering bills during the closing days of the session, and a two-thirds vote is required in either house to change their decision.[16] In New York and Nebraska the rules committees have similar roles. The rules committees used in Kentucky differ in that they are not established until the last fifteen days of the session and they are larger, sometimes including half or more of the legislators. The membership is carefully chosen, however, to include a preponderance of legislators on whom the leadership can depend, and in practice the rules committee appears to give the leadership as tight a control over legislative business as is possible in other states. In North Carolina a calendar committee is sometimes set up late in the session to serve the same purpose of establishing priorities and expediting consideration of favored bills. These rules committees illustrate how mechanical features of the legislature, which may seem highly technical to the student, can serve the purposes of political control. In these various states the rules committee has been utilized by dominant groups in the legislature to assure that they can maintain orderly control of the process during the hectic closing days of the session. It is a negative power capable of blocking measures that those in authority oppose. It is also a positive power in certain states where the committee can report out a bill that has been buried by a standing committee. The rules committee, when it has such broad powers, is an instrument of control—for the governor in Alabama, for a dominant rural clique in Florida, for the majority Republican party in New York, and for the dominant faction of the Democratic party in Kentucky.

Another type of leadership committee is often called a steering or policy committee and represents the leaders of a single party. It may be organized formally or simply operate in practice. This is the group that meets, often with the governor, to plan party strategy. The majority party—particularly if it is the governor's party —is more likely to have regular meetings of leaders from both houses than is the minority. In Illinois, for example, Republican leaders met weekly with the Republican governor during the 1953-60 period, while the Democratic leaders held no regular bicameral meetings.[17] There are occasions where more formal organizations exist. The Republicans in the Maine House, for example, have a policy committee consisting of one representative from each county. The Rhode Island Republicans have a policy committee consisting of leaders from both branches of the legislature and certain members of the state central committee, though it has not functioned with consistent success.[18] In general it appears that such formal institutionalization of party leadership in the legislatures is the exception rather than the rule. Obviously, where parties are strong, the leaders of a party will usually work closely together, and if they have the responsibilities of a majority they may even meet regularly with their counterparts in the other house. The smaller a minority party is and the less its responsibility for the legislative program, the less organized its leadership will be.

In some states the legislative council might also be described as a legislative committee. These councils, which sometimes have other titles, are found in thirty-six of the states. These organizations are often thought of primarily as research agencies, and they usually have staffs to study the substantive problems referred to them by the legislature. In about twenty states the legislative council has a more significant policy function; on the basis of staff studies, it plans a legislative program and recommends it to the legislature. Some or all of the elected leaders of the legislature are usually ex-officio members of the councils, often along with other legislators.

The councils vary greatly in their functions and effectiveness. In some states they have become instruments of gubernatorial leadership, while in others they serve to develop an alternative program to the governor's. The effectiveness of some councils is limited because of sharp partisan divisions among the members, while others are effective tools of majority party control. There is always the possibility that the legislative members of a council will not agree with the recommendations of professional staff members. From the viewpoint of legislative leaders, the potential of the council is considerable as long as they have control over its recommendations. The recommendations of the council can be developed carefully during the period between sessions, and they can be buttressed with staff studies that may give them greater weight in the legislature.[19]

The Party Caucus

Where a single party predominates, there is little reason for calling caucuses. In the two-party states, the caucus has proved to be a useful but not an inevitable feature of strong party leadership. In some states the majority leadership apparently finds it unnecessary to hold regular meetings of the rank-and-file members in order to give them the word on pending legislation. Some legislative leaders, like most congressional leaders, may believe that it is easier to maintain disciplined control and avoid intra-party debate and dissension if caucuses are held only rarely.

Even among the two-party states, caucuses vary considerably in frequency and importance. Since they are a matter of custom and convenience, it is difficult to describe accurately at any given time how important a role caucuses play in state legislatures. The majority party is more likely to hold caucuses than the minority, particularly if the minority membership is relatively small. In a number of states the caucus only meets once at the start of the legislature to nominate the Speaker or president pro tem and the floor leader.

A survey conducted more than ten years ago showed that some form of caucus was used by the majority party in most of the two-party states (categories C and D), but that in only about half of these did it meet frequently. In several states the caucus met every week or even daily, while in others it met more irregularly as important issues came up. Minority caucuses were found in most but not all the states where the majority held caucuses, but there were a few cases where minority caucuses were more frequent. Usually caucuses are limited to issues of particular importance to the party leadership, which uses this technique to gain more votes for a measure that may be in trouble; though the membership may be influenced by the pleas of leadership or a vote of the group, caucus decisions seldom appear to be binding on the individual legislators.[20]

There are a few states, however, in which the caucus of one or both parties dominates the legislative process. These examples are not typical; rather they show the potential of the caucus as an instrument for achieving party unity. The Republican Senate caucus in New Jersey was described several years ago as "without doubt the most powerful majority party caucus in any state legislative chamber."[21] The Republicans maintained control of the twenty-one-member, rural-dominated state Senate, even during the eight years of Democratic Governor Robert Meyner's administration. The caucus meets daily and decides which bills may be brought to the Senate floor. In recent years as few as six or seven Republican senators have been able to block Democratic administration bills from reaching the Senate floor for a vote. The Republicans have also had a strong caucus in the Assembly. Democratic Governor Meyner made the caucus system the target of his criticism during both campaigns for office, but was unable to prevent its use by Republicans, though the Democrats did gain control of the Assembly during Meyner's second term. The New Jersey caucus, particularly in the Senate, has been a device for assuring Republican unity and also maintaining rural dominance over the party.[22]

The caucus has been an instrument of unity for both Connecticut parties, especially in the Senate. A participant describes the Democratic Senate caucus:

> The caucus of senators, which takes place daily, is the scene of some protracted disputes and debates on bills, but when the senators leave their caucus to come to the floor it is rare indeed for the disputes of the inner chamber to be brought out in Senate debate and rarer still for members to desert in a roll call.
>
> In the daily caucus—to which is normally devoted far more time than that spent on the floor of the Senate—the procedure is to review the day's calendar of bills and to come to agreement on the party stand on all bills. All senators attend their respective caucuses, as do the state chairmen of the parties.

There may be perfunctory discussion or a debate that lasts for hours. On most issues a vote is taken, but on some there is so much disagreement that the members agree to vote independently. On issues of concern to the governor he will send a representative (usually the state chairman) to his party's caucus to explain why strong party support for the measure is necessary.[23]

In the neighboring states of Massachusetts and Rhode Island frequent caucuses also play a part in maintaining party unity. These three states are ones where party unity on roll calls is particularly high. The caucus system is a contributing factor but certainly not the major cause of this unity. In these states socio-economic factors have led to the creation of parties that are homogeneous and unified enough so that it is possible for a caucus system in the legislature to produce even greater unity on roll calls.

In the California Assembly, caucuses have been frequent but informal and much less effective. Caucuses are not used in the Senate, where party lines have been less meaningful and the parties have been splintered. Prior to 1937 caucuses were not held in most Assembly sessions, not even for organizational purposes. Democratic caucuses began in 1937; under a Democratic administration elected in 1938 they were sometimes held in the governor's office. In recent years they have met weekly to discuss measures that might become party policy but have not sought to bind participants to the majority viewpoint and have not publicized decisions unless there was unanimity. The Republican caucus in the Assembly grew out of informal meetings of freshman legislators. Its meetings likewise produce more unity but few examples of party unanimity on important measures. In both parties the caucus serves a social as well as a legislative purpose which may have some effect in generating party harmony.[24]

In states where the dominant party has been split into factions, factional caucuses sometimes assume importance, though they are likely to be more ephemeral than party caucuses. A survey of a dozen years ago, for example, showed that factional caucuses played some role in six one-party states.[25]

The Standing Committees

Students visiting Congress or the state legislatures who are disappointed by the lack of exciting activity on the floor are always told that "the real work goes on in committees." In Congress this is undoubtedly true. The standing committees act independently on legislation and determine whether and in what form bills reach the floor. Committees are able to maintain this independent role because their members have developed expert knowledge on the subject and an independence from the control of party leaders, both by virtue of long and inviolate tenure on the committees. The congressional committees are independent sources of power. It is often true that the "real work" goes on in state legislative committees, but it is by no means certain that these committees exercise an independence comparable to those in Congress. They are more often important as instruments of control for other political forces.

There are several reasons why legislative standing committees are but pale shadows of their congressional counterparts. In most states the legislature meets for only two or three months every other year, and important legislation is often introduced late in the session, giving the committees little time for careful review. We have already described the system of channeling important bills into a few committees dominated by relatively few legislators. The number of committees in the legislatures has gradually been cut to an average of about twenty-two in each house, but there are still states where the number is excessive. Whether the number is large or small, the workload tends to be unbalanced, with one group of members who are loyal to the leadership overworked, while the less favored legislators may find themselves on a number of committees that do little or nothing. The committees usually do not have the staff assistance that is necessary for an informed review of bills.

Not only do legislative committees lack the time, staff, and resources to do their work carefully, but they lack the stature to do it independently A basic purpose of legislative committees is to permit specialization. This requires that members serve on committees long enough to acquire familiarity in depth with the subject matter of the committee. In some states relatively few legislators serve for more than three or four terms. A study in 1950 showed that in eight states less than one-fifth of the committee chairmen had served in the legislature more than three terms.[26] A Missouri study recently showed that chairmen of important committees were sometimes freshmen in the legislature and were often serving their first terms on the committee. It also showed that chairmen often shifted from one committee to another.[27] In most legislative bodies a member with a thorough knowledge of his subject stands the best chance of being influential. The committee that is composed of amateurs is not likely to carry much weight in legislative deliberations. We have already noted that the seniority principle, though often observed in committee assignments, is not an iron-clad rule as in Congress. The dominant leaders on a committee may be removed in the next session if they act too independently. The committee, in short, is not a stable base on which legislators may build their power.

Let us assume that a group of legislators from urban communities win a majority of seats on a municipalities committee and decide to use this committee to reshape the legislative proposals of a rural group dominating the legislature. They cannot depend on the assistance of a research staff. Important bills concerning urban problems may be sidetracked to other committees or taken over by an all-powerful rules committee late in the session. In the next legislature half of their members may have retired or been defeated while the other half are transferred to other committees by the leadership.

The contrast between congressional and state legislative committees is well illustrated by their different approaches to the budget. At the national level the appropriations committees are divided into subcommittees, made up of congressmen who have often specialized in the work of the defense department or foreign aid, for example, for many years. Assisted by trained staffs, they spend months reviewing the budget requests, policies, and performance of an agency before approving or revising its requests. The actions of the House Appropriations Committee are carefully reviewed by its counterpart in the Senate. In some state legislatures, staff facilities are available for the committees and the budget is studied for several weeks. In Texas there is even a legislative budget bureau, well staffed, that prepares its own budget proposal on the basis of requests from various departments.

A more typical situation is that in Illinois. The appropriations committees have two months or more to consider the budget, and they hold extensive hearings at which agency heads appear to explain and justify requests. But the committees lack both the staff and the desire for independent scrutiny of a budget that has already been carefully prepared by the administration. Committee members may raise a few questions, often on trivial points, but the hearings are largely a formality. The members make no serious effort to challenge the administration's budget request, though they may scrutinize more carefully appropriation bills not included in that budget. Moreover, the committee does not use appropriations hearings as a means of questioning departmental policies and programs.[28]

In some states the legislative review of the budget is even more cursory. The governor will deliver his budget to the legislature on Monday. Members of the responsible committee will have a day or two to read and digest several hundred pages of figures. Tuesday the budget director will appear before the committee to answer questions. Wednesday, perhaps after listening to requests from interest groups for more funds, the committee will meet in executive session and approve the budget, often with one or two minor changes.

The fact that legislative committees are seldom *independent* sources of power does not mean that they are impotent or insignificant in the legislative process. The committees may be an important means through which some party or faction maintains its control in the legislature. The dominant party or faction normally has a majority on all the committees or at least the important ones. Members of committees are picked either by the presiding officer or by a committee controlled by the legislative leadership, and the floor leaders or other legislative leaders may themselves chair important committees.

In a two-party state the majority party normally has all committee chairmanships, and the ratio of Republicans to Democrats on each committee usually approximates that in the legislature, though the ratio may not be adhered to as rigidly as is done in Congress, and the minority sometimes has to fight for its proportionate share of seats. In Illinois the size of committees is varied to maintain a standard party ratio while complying with the preferred committee assignments of most members. In some states where party affiliation is less significant or where a single party dominates, however, the minority party is given the chairmanship of some committees where it has only minority representation.

In California the legislature was organized on a nonpartisan basis from 1913 until the mid-thirties, and party affiliation did not determine committee assignments or chairmanships. In the Senate this practice has continued generally until the present; most recently the majority party has had majorities on all committees, but chairmanships have gone to members of either party strictly on the basis of seniority. In the Assembly recently the majority Democratic party has controlled nearly all committees, but the Republicans have chaired about one-fourth of them. This practice occurs sometimes because the Speaker has promised chairmanships to members of the minority party as a means of getting their votes to win election.[29] In the Kentucky Senate there are usually just enough committees to give each senator, including the minority Republicans, a chairmanship. In Vermont, where the legislature is overwhelmingly Republican, chairmen are picked on the basis of ability, experience, and seniority; this means that some chairmen—even of relatively important committees—are Democrats. A few years ago, when the Democrats were badly outnumbered in the Oregon legislature, they were occasionally given chairmanships of important committees. Though party organization is fairly strong in Washington, the minority party there often holds a few less important chairmanships. It is doubtful whether a chairman who is not guaranteed tenure and who is politically outnumbered both on the committee and in the legislature gains much power from his position.

The Minnesota legislature provides a good example of how a dominant faction can exercise its control through committees. Though it is nonpartisan, the Minnesota legislature is organized into a Conservative and a Liberal caucus. The Conservative caucus has controlled the Senate and usually the House during the last few decades. By choosing the House speaker and the Senate committee on committees the dominant faction is assured control of the committee on rules and other key committees in both houses. In 1959, for example, the Senate Conservative caucus had a complete monopoly on the committee on committees and the committee on rules; on other major committees it held the chairmanship and a majority of members much greater than its share of Senate seats.[30]

A recent study of the Florida legislature by Beth and Havard provides an excellent illustration of how a dominant clique, in this case leaders of a conservative rural group, can maintain control through committees. The rural wing has a constitutional advantage based on the apportionment system and various limits on gubernatorial power. The committees in Florida have enough prestige to make their favorable or unfavorable recommendations usually effective on the floor of the legislature. The committee chairmen frequently dominate committees more from personal influence and skill than from formal powers. When the legislative leaders have been picked by the ruling conservative group, they have stacked the key committees with a solid majority of legislators who either come from rural counties or have worked closely with the rural wing. Actually the Florida legislature is dominated by an interlocking directorate of a dozen or more members in each house who hold the most important legislative posts and serve as chairmen or members of the key committees. In 1959, for example, a group of thirteen senators (out of thirty-eight) held forty-nine seats, including all chairmanships, on the six most important committees.[31]

It is frequently a practice for legislative committees to be heavily weighted with members who have some personal interest in the subjects under the committee's jurisdiction. This does guarantee considerable committee familiarity with the subject and perhaps a degree of independence from control by legislative leadership. It may also guarantee that certain lobbyists receive highly preferential treatment in these committees. Perhaps the most frequent practice is to place only lawyers on the judiciary committee. In some cases all lawyers serve on the judiciary committee, and North Carolina has even solved the problem of a surplus of lawyers by creating two judiciary committees in each house. When a committee is likely to deal with legislation regulating a particular interest, the composition of the committee becomes particularly important. The Senate banking committee in Alabama, for example, a few years ago had a majority of bankers. The alcoholic beverage control committee in the Maryland House recently consisted mostly of tavern keepers, beer distributors, and lawyers representing liquor interests. Florida committees dealing with citrus products and forestry have been made up almost entirely of citrus growers and representatives of the forestry interests. In a recent session of the Kentucky legislature all members of the House who were veterans were put on the veterans' committee, all insurance agents were on the insurance committee, and most of those on the agricultural committee were farmers.

At best this practice may simply guarantee that legislators will serve on committees where they can contribute the most knowledge and experience. At worst the system can turn a committee into a powerful lobby influential in passing legislation favorable to a single interest and, more important, unchallengeable in its veto of bills opposed by that interest. This is actually one aspect of a broader problem, the combination legislator-lobbyist. Congressmen share with state legislators the problem of separating group and business interests from their responsibility as representatives of the voter, but the legislator's temptations are likely to be greater because he is only a part-time legislator but is often a full-time lawyer, insurance agent, businessman, or farmer. The state legislature is called upon, more frequently than Congress, to pass bills regulating businesses and professions, often favoring one interest at the direct expense of the other. It is common practice for legislators with the most direct personal interest in certain bills to be most active in committee and on the floor in promoting or defeating them.

How important is committee action on a bill? In most states the committees play a decisive role in killing bills that do not meet their approval; of course, not all bills favorably reported by a committee become law or even pass one house. In a few states the committees are required to report out all bills, usually within a time limit. Though this system theoretically limits the committee's veto power, which might be exercised arbitrarily, the system does not work well whether it is used or abused. Frequently committees get around the requirement by reporting out all pigeonholed bills on the last day of the session, reporting them with a motion to recommit, or perhaps even ignoring the requirement. In a state where the requirement is adhered to, it can lead to situations like that in Massachusetts where 3,697 bills were introduced and reported out in 1955, but only one-quarter of them passed.[32] Without a doubt many bills are introduced that should never be released by committee to clog the legislative machinery.

One way of controlling committees without removing their discretionary power is to make it easier for rank-and-file legislators to discharge a bill from committee. In practice this is seldom done, and in some states it is rare for a single bill to be discharged during a session. This is not so much because it is difficult but because legislators traditionally respect the authority and discretion of committees. Since this is so often a matter of custom, changes in the rules might not in fact encourage the discharge of bills. In Illinois the discharge petition is sometimes used to pass noncontroversial bills that have been overlooked in committee, but it is seldom successful in the passage of controversial measures —though the threat of a discharge motion may prove effective in liberating a bill.[33] In practice when strong leadership dominates both the rank-and-file and the committees, there is little reason why a majority in the legislature should seek to liberate bills from committee. In some states the committees kill bills primarily by pigeonholing them, while in others it is often customary to file an unfavorable report. Bills so reported are usually defeated. In Florida a bill unfavorably reported requires a two-thirds vote to pass and is most unlikely to get it in the face of committee disapproval.

The role played by committees varies from state to state. A careful study of the Illinois legislature by Steiner and Gove concluded that the committees there seldom play a decisive role in the legislative process. In Illinois the committees never pigeonhole a bill if the sponsor presses for a hearing and a vote on it. Bills die in committee entirely because the sponsor decides not to attempt to bring the bill to the floor. Moreover, only about three per cent of the bills are reported out by committee with an unfavorable recommendation; when this occurs, the bill rarely becomes law. Committee members generally pass the buck to the legislature as a whole. Moreover, the committee seldom makes controversial amendments in the bill. The committee's role is further reduced by two other practices: noncontroversial legislation is often passed by suspending the rules and avoiding referral to committee, and late in the session even important legislation is often not referred to committee in the second house.[34]

In Illinois the committees play a minor role partly because they lack the time and staff to consider legislation carefully. Interim commissions have been used increasingly to give more careful study to important issues. A major reason for the subsidiary role of committees is the importance of parties in the Illinois legislature. On issues of concern to the administration, party lines are likely to be drawn in the committee, and consequently the majority party has little difficulty reporting the bill favorably. Committees play a smaller role in Illinois when the same party controls the governorship and both houses; under these conditions the committee will report out administration-approved bills almost automatically, while the sponsor of a bill who has been unable to get administration support may not even seek a hearing on his bill.

Where the leadership of a party or a faction has strong control over a legislature, the committees are least likely to have an independent role. In some states the leadership uses key committees to advance or defeat legislation; in a state like Illinois the committees play a more perfunctory role and the leadership usually counts on passing or defeating bills on the floor. There is considerable variety from state to state in the proportion of bills reported by committee. In most states, however, and particularly where the legislature is under strong leadership, the committees are not *independent* centers of power and discretion but are simply the stage on which outside groups—governors, party leaders, and lobbyists—fight their battles or negotiate their compromises.

Organization and Power

The close observer of the legislative process soon learns that legislative institutions often do not perform the function that their titles suggest. There is often a paper caucus that meets only biennially. There are frequently committees that do not receive bills on the subjects implied by their titles or that rubber stamp those bills they do receive. A lieutenant governor may be powerful in one state and a figurehead in the next. The similarity of terms in the various legislatures—rules committees, the Speaker, the caucus—is deceptive because these institutions mean something different from state to state.

In examining any legislative body, the student must assume that certain individuals or groups are most influential and must search these out. In a strong two-party state, they are most likely to be party leaders; elsewhere leaders of factions or representatives of the governor may stand out. In any state legislature, but particularly where the parties are weak, lobbyists may be strong. The organizational structure can be best understood as an instrument of leadership. The student who has identified leaders in a legislative body may then investigate which organizational devices are used to control the legislative process. Actual leadership usually rests in the hands of those who hold the formal positions of authority: the speaker, floor leader, and sometimes the chairmen of key committees. Through control over procedure and committee assignments and often through their influence with the governor, these leaders usually exercise considerable power. Their institutional techniques vary. Leaders in one state may use the caucus just as effectively and to the same end as leaders in another state use a strong rules committee. In some states, but not in all, the leadership operates largely through the standing committees, assigning important bills arbitrarily to committees packed with dependable legislators to assure prompt approval or certain burial of the bills.

By and large it is true to say that the legislators are organized for strong leadership. The legislature, and particularly its committees, are not organized to provide careful deliberation on legislation. Usually the sessions are too short, and the legislators too poorly staffed, to permit that. Seldom is power dispersed so widely among committees as it is in Congress. By and large it is true to say that the legislators are organized for strong leadership, and this leadership often emanates from the governor's office.

FIVE

THE GOVERNOR AS A LEGISLATOR

If you think we are worked by strings,
Like a Japanese marionette,
You don't understand these things:
It is simply Court etiquette.

—THE MIKADO

The student who has been brought up to believe in separation of powers as the fundamental principle of American government often finds it difficult to understand the legislative role that the chief executive, both national and state, has played in the twentieth century. It is not just a negative role, as embodied in the veto power. The chief executive is frequently, though not always in the states, the most powerful single force in the legislative process. The gubernatorial candidate offers the electorate not merely more honest, efficient government but also a legislative program. Implicit in his campaign is the promise, often a rash promise, that he will secure the enactment of this program by the legislature. From the voter's viewpoint the governor has a program and perhaps a record of legislation that is usually far better known than the program and record of the local legislative candidate.

The legislator during his term of office has many glimpses of the governor as a legislative leader. These are not merely the occasions on which the governor reads a message to the legislature or returns a bill with his veto. During Huey Long's day the Louisiana legislator frequently saw the governor on the floor of the legislature personally lobbying for his bills, while a recent Kentucky governor sometimes sat beside the presiding officer during critical roll calls. On other occasions the governor or one of his aides may be sitting in the balcony and keeping track of the vote on roll calls. More frequently the legislator is called into the governor's office and asked to support a bill, or else he is buttonholed by the floor leader and informed that the governor is vitally concerned about a measure. In the preceding chapters the reader has caught an occasional glimpse of the governor moving quietly behind the scenes, and the discerning reader has probably felt that the governor has more influence on the events already described than has yet been admitted. In this chapter it is time to bring the governor out from the shadows and examine his legislative role.

With a consistency that may have begun to bore the reader we have pointed out that legislative politics varies tremendously from state to state, however similar the legislative bodies may appear to be on the surface. There is a pattern in this variety, however, the outline of which derives from the degree of two-party competition in the various states. When we look at the governor in the American states we find a similar variation for the same reason. In addition we find that the authority and operating methods of the governor vary for constitutional reasons and also because of tradition and habit. Finally, we discover that the personalities and abilities of successive governors in a single state may be different enough to have a marked effect on their legislative roles. Heretofore, in making generalizations we have been out on the proverbial limb; in this chapter we are dangling precariously from the twigs.

Formal Powers of the Governor

There is a clear distinction between the gubernatorial powers that are formal and often constitutional and those that are informal and often political. We may start with the former, which are easier to describe and which apply more generally to the various states. The first constitutional source of the governor's authority is his responsibility for making periodic reports to the legislature on the affairs of the state. Just as the annual state of the union message provided for in the Constitution gives the President an opportunity for presenting his program to the nation, so the governor uses the occasion of his annual or biennial message to present a program for legislative enactment. Like the President, the governor may follow this up with more detailed messages on specific subjects. Moreover, it is increasingly likely that major legislation of concern to the governor will be drafted in a state agency and then introduced by one of the governor's spokesmen in the legislature. The governor in the past has not always played such an important role as the initiator of legislation. The growing multitude and complexity of governmental problems have put a premium on expertise; the poorly staffed, part-time legislators are seldom prepared to initiate major statewide legislative programs. So obvious is the need for executive initiative that it would probably have developed without any constitutional excuse; nevertheless, the provisions for a gubernatorial message provided a useful seed from which the modern program of the administration has grown.

The governor is not merely a coordinator of legislative proposals drafted by experts. His message to the legislature is a political document of major importance. If he is a skillful governor and particularly if he has

107

learned the art of capturing public support, the governor's message may become the rallying point for the various forces that he is able to enlist on his behalf. The point cannot be too strongly made that in the American states today the governor holds the initiative; he proposes and the legislature disposes. It is rare that an important legislative measure is passed that has not been initiated by the executive. The governor's monopoly in this area is probably greater than the President's; a closer comparison might be with the President's initiative on foreign policy legislation.

Closely related to legislative initiative is the preparation of the budget. In some states the governor must share this authority with a commission including other elective officers or legislators, but in most states the governor has exclusive control. He is often handicapped, however, by legislation earmarking large portions of tax revenue for specific spending programs. In some states the governor's budget usually passes with little difficulty, but in others it is the most hotly contested issue in a legislative session. In these latter states the budget may frequently be cut, but it is much less likely to be raised appreciably and in a few states the legislature is not permitted to increase appropriations.

Though there is no precise way of estimating the impact of gubernatorial initiative, a number of studies have shown that most governors have a high "batting average" on the measures proposed in their messages. These averages have ranged from slightly over 50 per cent in Alabama to over 90 per cent for some governors in Virginia and Kentucky.[1] Sometimes a deadlock between a governor and legislature of opposing parties may lead to much lower figures, and even where the percentage is high the measures that pass are sometimes watered-down versions of gubernatorial recommendations. We cannot be precise about the success of the governor; we can only emphasize that he holds the initiative and frequently secures enactment of a large proportion of his recommendations.

The governor's power to call special sessions, while generally less important, may at times be of considerable significance. The special session is potentially an important tool of the governor in those states (a large proportion of the total) where the governor alone is empowered to call such a session and to determine the subjects that may be considered during it. The session may serve a variety of useful purposes. If unacceptable amendments have been added to an administration-backed bill, the governor may veto it and call a special session to pass a revised bill. Likewise he may call a special session to focus attention on some subject concerning which the legislature has failed to act; this may intensify pressure on the legislators. He may threaten to call a special session if the legislature shelves one of his bills. The governor may deliberately postpone an important issue until a special session meets in order to secure its careful consideration free from other pressures. In 1956 the Kentucky governor persuaded the legislature to adjourn four weeks early and then convened two special sessions to deal exclusively with revenue and appropriations. Perhaps an extreme example of gubernatorial manipulation of special sessions was provided by the same Kentucky governor, who announced that he would call a special session to deal with the issue of expanded unemployment compensation if a majority of the legislators in each house would first notify him by letter that they would vote for the terms of a measure he favored; they did not, and he did not convene the legislature.

While the governor's positive influence over legislation is considerable, his negative authority is massive. In every state except North Carolina the governor has the veto power, and in most states it requires a vote of more than a majority of the legislature to override the veto. A study published in 1950 showed that slightly more than 5 per cent of bills passed by state legislatures were vetoed, and only 1 or 2 per cent of the vetoes were overridden. Actually the national percentage of overridden vetoes conceals wide variations, and in a single year most of the vetoes that are overridden may be concentrated in a handful of states where there are partisan or factional cleavages between governor and legislature. In a few states vetoes are almost never successfully challenged. Only three vetoes have been overridden in Illinois since 1870, only one in Pennsylvania from 1900 to 1950, and only thirteen in Michigan from 1909 to 1947, for example. Overridden vetoes are almost unknown in New York, Iowa, Kansas, and Louisiana, among others.[2] In two recent sessions the Kentucky legislature overrode vetoes on only two bills, both raising the expense allowance of legislators.

There are several reasons why the governor in most states can nearly always make his veto stick. His political power is usually great enough so that he can maintain the support of the one-third or two-fifths necessary to uphold a veto. Moreover, a large proportion of bills are passed in the closing days of the session, and on these the governor can exercise his veto after the legislature has adjourned. In two recent Illinois legislative sessions about 90 per cent of the governor's vetoes came after adjournment. In Alaska, however, the legislature holds an additional session to deal with bills vetoed after adjournment. Finally it should be noted that the threat of a veto can often forestall passage of a bill or force the elimination of objectionable amendments from the bill.

The governor has the power of executive amendment in four states: Alabama, Virginia, Massachusetts, and New Jersey. As an alternative to vetoing a bill, he can resubmit it to the legislature with proposed changes; the legislature may adopt the bill with his amendments or readopt its originally proposed bill. In the two southern states the legislatures have usually approved the governor's amendments, while in Massachusetts the governor has been less successful and in New Jersey the device is relatively new. In Alabama and Massachusetts particularly, the executive amendment has been used more often than the veto on policy questions. It is a more flexible instrument and may give the governor a more positive and more significant role in the legislative process than does the veto.[3]

In forty-one states the governor has an item veto on appropriations bills, and in several of these states he has the authority to reduce appropriations items.[4] Potentially this is a significant grant of power, although in some states the governor's political authority in the legislature is great enough to prevent many objectionable items from being included in the budget.

The constitution not only grants the governor significant power in the legislative process, but in many states it imposes important limitations on his influence. About one-third of the states limit the governor to four years in office at a single time (either in a single term or two two-year terms), and a few others limit him to eight years. The four-year limit is characteristic of almost every southern and border state. The consequence of this limitation is that during the second half of his administration the governor has declining influence in the legislature. Both the promises and threats that he may make appear less potent to the legislators. Another constitutional limitation on his authority is the fact that in many states a large number of the most important administrative officials are publicly elected and hence not directly responsible to him.

These officials are likely to control patronage in their own departments, to make their own recommendations to the legislature, and perhaps to win an independent following in the legislature. The skillful governor may be able to control other elected officials through the budget and through the exercise of his personal political authority, but his formal powers and often his informal influence are frequently limited when he must share administrative responsibility with many elected officials.

The Governor as Political Leader

It is relatively easy to discuss the governor's formal powers in terms that are widely applicable, but his political leadership is most varied and is largely dependent on the nature of two-party politics in the state. His opportunity for party leadership is greatest in a two-party state where his party has a majority in both branches of the legislature. The reader will recall from Chapter II that there are comparatively few states in which this prototype of gubernatorial leadership is regularly found. In a two-party state the governor, particularly if he is a Democrat, is just as likely to find the opposition party controlling one or both legislative branches. The third situation is one in which a single party is so dominant that, paradoxically, the governor has little opportunity to exercise party leadership; in the absence of a strong opposition the majority party splinters into factions and personal cliques.

In the strongly competitive two-party states where the governor's party has a majority in both branches, his legislative influence may be vast; if his party lacks that majority, the governor who is an effective political leader can still bargain with the opposition from a position of strength. Where a single party predominates, the governor may be able to organize a faction loyal to him and large enough to control the legislature, but this is more difficult than maintaining a readymade political majority. Factions are transitory and fade quickly, especially in the southern and border states where the governor has a single term. Where factions have replaced parties, the apportionment system frequently leads to legislative control by a rural faction while the governor owes greater allegiance to the urban centers, which are providing an increasing proportion of the popular vote. It is not uncommon for divided government in this sense to flourish in one-party states.

Political leadership can mean many things: publicly advocating a program, planning strategy with legislative leaders, manipulating patronage to achieve legislative goals. All governors use these and similar techniques to varying degrees in attempting to influence the legislature, but whether this is party, factional, or purely personal leadership depends on the state's political environment.

One of the major sources of the governor's power is his influence over public opinion. In the last few decades the press conference, radio, television, and modern transportation have changed the nature of political leadership. The governor, like the President, has gained a larger role in the legislative process primarily because of his ability to dramatize his stand on issues and enlist public support through modern communications media. New York, for example, has had powerful governors, from Roosevelt to Rockefeller, who drew their strength largely from an ability to touch a responsive chord in the public mind.

Like the President, though on a smaller scale, the governor has a great advantage over legislators in influencing public opinion. What he says is news and commands attention in the press, perhaps on the front page. He can gain radio and television time, usually without cost. Unlike the legislators, he can speak with a single voice and focus attention on a single program that he believes should have legislative priority. The typical governor's day is filled with speeches, and if he chooses he can use these occasions to sell a legislative program to the people. Many governors have ignored these opportunities or proved inept in exploiting them, but the governor's potential influence on public opinion is enormous.

Most governors come into office with a platform that provides the basis for their legislative program. In a two-party state the governor must run on his party's platform, which may or may not be fully satisfactory to him. In fact, like a presidential candidate, he generally picks his own issues from the platform for use during the campaign. In a one-party state the gubernatorial candidate has maximum freedom to create his own platform, however general or specific, in the primary. In either case the governor's program usually assumes more definite shape when he presents his first message to the legislature.[5] The governor has the initiative in the legislative process. During the campaign he is developing and promoting his policies while most legislative candidates are shaking hands with the voters and discussing a few local issues. When the legislators arrive at the capital they find a ready-made program waiting for them in the governor's office.

Two points should be made clear about the governor's public role in the legislative process. First, though his role has grown in recent decades, it still varies tremendously with differences in skill and personality. Second, in most states the public does not look upon him primarily as a party leader but as the state leader. He gains public support because of his skill in formulating and presenting his policies and not automatically because he is leader of the majority party.

In addition to his public role of influencing opinion,

the governor who is an effective legislative leader plays an important behind-the-scenes role. Perhaps the best test of his control in the legislature is his influence over the choice of the elected leaders and key committee members. In a two-party state when his party has a legislative majority a strong governor will be able to choose the top leaders and then will work closely with them in filling the important committee slots. In some states the governor may find it impossible or at least unwise to replace a Speaker, for example, who has served many years, but normally the legislative leaders do not acquire such tenure.

In a state dominated by a single party the governor's influence is less predictable. In the last chapter we mentioned, for example, the technique used by a rural group in the Florida legislature of selecting the Speaker so far in advance that the governor has no influence. In Alabama, on the other hand, the governor's choice of legislative leaders is almost always accepted without question by the members. On those rare occasions when the Alabama governor makes no designation, the legislature sometimes finds it difficult to choose among a multitude of candidates. The designated leaders are normally expected to be loyal to the governor. The incumbent Speaker in Alabama has been known to avoid seeking re-election to the post because he could not support the governor-elect's platform. The power of choosing committees in the Alabama Senate has sometimes been taken away from a lieutenant governor who was not in sympathy with the governor.[6] While in some states, like Alabama, the governor's influence over the choice of leaders appears to be a matter of custom, in other one-party states the governor's effort to choose leaders will be the first step in his struggle to form a loyal faction in the legislature, and his success or failure may tell much about the fate of his legislative program.

The legislative leaders and particularly the Speaker of the lower house exercise wide powers, described in the preceding chapter. If these leaders are men with whom the governor can work closely, his legislative program has a head start; if not, his program is in trouble.

The governor usually meets with his legislative leaders at least weekly and more often in the busy final weeks of the session. He is likely to play a more direct role in planning legislative strategy than the President does. The sessions are usually much shorter than congressional sessions, and in their closing days legislative business assumes priority over all other gubernatorial duties. Though operating methods vary, the governor is likely to talk personally with some of the rank-and-file legislators about important bills that may be in jeopardy. He may appear personally before a party caucus or testify at a committee hearing in behalf of his program.

The governor must rely on others both to keep the legislators informed and to win their support for the administration's bills. The presiding officers and floor leaders in the legislature bear the brunt of this work. They may notify committee members of their party about administration bills in time to assure a favorable committee vote. They may report the administration's views formally in a caucus or informally in private conferences with legislators. At least in the larger states, there are one or more members of the governor's staff who devote most of their time during the sessions to liaison with the legislature, its rank-and-file members as well as the leaders. In Connecticut the Democratic state chairman, John Bailey, regularly attended party caucuses to present the case for legislation of importance to the Democratic governor. In Illinois the Democratic governor may receive strong support from lobbyists for the Chicago city government. Particularly in states where pressure groups have a close alliance with one or another party, lobbyists for these groups may work for parts of the governor's program of no direct concern to them in return for gubernatorial support on other measures.

The Governor's Party Sanctions

What arguments can the governor or his representatives use to persuade reluctant legislators to support the administration's bills or to vote against those it opposes? Often it is enough to describe the reasons for the administration's stand; legislators respect expert knowledge and recognize that members of the administration are often better informed than they are. If these arguments alone are not persuasive, the governor in a two-party state has other arguments and inducements that he can use with members of his own party. In some states party loyalty is a binding force. It may often be enough for the governor to tell legislators that a bill is a high-priority administration measure, that the governor's prestige is at stake. Under these conditions most legislators in the governor's party will vote as he requests unless conflicting pressure from other sources is unbearable.

The governor often has sanctions that can be applied, or held in reserve as a threat, to members of his own party. They may want important committee assignments or even aspire to leadership posts, over which he has some control. In some cases the governor's influence over local party organizations is great enough so that he can block the renomination of dissident legislators. New York is an example of a state where the administration's influence over county and district chairmen is strong enough so that they are often enlisted to put pressure on recalcitrant legislators.[7] Since the legislator is nominated by primary in most states, the local organization is not always able to control his renomination, but it may exercise some control over his political future by assisting candidates to run against him in the primary or by failing to work for him in the general election. One of the weaknesses of the President as a party leader is that he rarely has any influence over the nomination of congressmen. Probably relatively few governors have such influence over legislators, but in some of the states with strong, tightly disciplined parties this is a potent sanction. A writer on Connecticut politics has provided examples of these sanctions in use. When the Republican Speaker in 1945 broke with other party leaders on a number of issues, he was denied nomination as lieutenant governor and in 1947 was re-moved as Speaker and given only trivial committee assignments. In 1948 the party leadership was able to block his nomination, and that of several supporters, to the legislature. Democratic legislators in that state, where the primary was not adopted until 1955 and is little used, have also found it difficult to win renomination after splitting with party leaders.[8]

The governor in a one-party state may be able to punish recalcitrant legislators by barring their path to important posts in the legislature, but he has much less opportunity to pose a threat to their renomination. In Chapter II we discussed the weakness of factionalism in legislative primaries; these are likely to be wide-open affairs in which the governor's influence is only occasionally powerful. In the southern and border states the one-term limitation means that the governor's only chance to influence nominations is during the mid-term election.

In theory the strongest sanction a governor can have over a legislator is control over his renomination and re-election. Though this sanction means little to the many legislators who plan to retire after a term or two, it is important to others. This is just partly a question of influence over renomination. The most important advantage enjoyed exclusively by the governor in a two-party state is that many members of his party recognize that their re-election is dependent on voter approval of the administration. The average legislator lacks the independent stature and the personal hold on his district that many congressmen have. He usually knows that if his constituents vote for his party's candidate for governor they will vote for him. This fact of political life is a major asset to the governor in keeping his party in line on legislation, but it is a limited asset. This is a factor that creates a fundamental attitude of party loyalty among legislators; it does not guarantee support for the governor on any particular bill. The governor finds it difficult to persuade a legislator that any single bill is vital to the life of the administration. Moreover, the governor realizes that constituents are ignorant of details in the legislator's voting record and are unlikely to punish the dissident member of a party by voting against him.

The governor's basic disadvantage in a one-party state is that legislators do not believe that their re-election is linked to the success of the administration. In this area factions are a poor substitute for parties because the voters do not consistently see a connection between the record of the administration and the factional alignments of legislators. At the risk of repetition, it is important to point out again that in the southern and border one-party states there is often little continuity between successive single-term administrations, and consequently the legislator's fate is even less related to that of the administration.

Patronage as a Sanction

Although the governor in a two-party state with a legislative majority has a major advantage over a governor in a one-party state, some of the outstanding examples of strong governors, capable of winning legislative enactment of their programs, are found in one-party states. Why? We have discussed some sources of power available to governors in all states, such as the virtual monopoly of expert knowledge in his administration and his opportunities to influence public opinion. Other important sources of his legislative influence are less publicized: the jobs, contracts, road projects, and other favors that a governor can offer a legislator, his friends, or his district. We will use the term patronage to describe not merely government jobs but this whole range of favors. Patronage is available in greater or lesser amounts for all governors to dispense. In two-party states patronage is likely to be one of the factors in maintaining party discipline, sometimes of critical importance and sometimes necessary only in marginal cases. In a one-party state, where the governor lacks the natural forces of party unity, patronage may become the crucial factor in securing his legislative program.[9]

In most states the dispensing of jobs offers the governor one of his best opportunities to influence legislators; this is more important to most governors than to the President. Job patronage is a risky weapon, however, a two-handled sword. Any appointment may disappoint more legislators than it pleases, and the unskilled governor may discover that normally loyal legislators are threatening to vote against him unless a certain appointment is made. Not all job patronage can be used for legislative purposes; the governor may have promised most of the available jobs (or perhaps more than are available) to secure support for his primary and election campaigns.

The number of available jobs differs greatly from state to state. In some states only a few jobs are covered by the merit system, while in about half a large proportion are included. Where there is an extensive merit system, the patronage jobs are like to be the top policy-making posts and the unskilled, casual labor such as is found in the highway department. Several years ago the number of patronage jobs in the Pennsylvania government was estimated at 35,000, while in Wisconsin there are only a handful of policy-making jobs not under the merit system. Where there are a number of other elected state officials, they usually fill the patronage slots in their own departments, sometimes leaving the governor with a small proportion of the patronage, as is the case in Florida, for example. In some states, even without an extensive merit system, there is a strong tradition against wholesale patronage appointments, a tradition that the governor may hesitate to break. The jobs available for the governor's use sometimes include those with private firms doing contract work for the state or with pressure groups or businesses active in lobbying. This least publicized form of job patronage is difficult to measure but is sometimes an important asset for the governor.

Without a doubt many governors find that job patronage is a colossal headache, causing them far more trouble than it is worth. It is nonetheless true that in many states a governor with political skill can advance his legislative program through the deft handling of the jobs at his disposal. While many appointments must be made at the start of the administration, the governor can sometimes maintain control over the legislator by the veiled threat to dismiss a constituent from a choice job if the legislator becomes disloyal.

The governor can also offer a wide variety of services and favors to the legislator's district. Roads are perhaps the most important, because a road is a concrete, visible governmental service valued by the constituent more than most state services. The legislator can probably win more votes by producing a road for his county than by his voting record or any or all of his other services. The state government must also determine where to locate parks, hospitals, colleges, and a variety of other services and institutions. In the case of all these services there are other factors that the governor may have to take into account: the reports of engineers, the needs of the communities, federal advice when there is federal aid, and perhaps campaign pledges that he has already made. We might argue that these projects should be distributed according to merit and need, but in fact governors are usually able to win legislative support by distributing some of them as a form of patronage.

A closely related power of the governor, though one not often described as patronage, is his control over local legislation. In the many states that lack home rule for cities or counties, a large number of bills must be passed by the legislature to deal with local problems. Though these are often completely noncontroversial, they may be of considerable importance to the locality and consequently to the local legislator. If the governor has sufficient influence in the legislature to block passage of such bills, he can use this threat to gain the support of individual legislators for his program. This is a technique that may be used equally by governors in two-party or one-party states.

Another form of patronage is the distribution of state contracts, whether for highway work, the supply of state liquor stores, the purchase of textbooks, the insurance of state buildings, or the bonding of state employees. Most contracts for these purposes must be let through competitive bidding, but in most states there are some types of contracts exempt from these regulations, and too often there are ways of avoiding or manipulating the legal provisions to favor a certain company. The specifications may be worded so as to fit only one firm, or a firm may be given advance notice of bids, for example. These forms of patronage, like the others, may be given to individuals who have provided campaign funds or political support in the past, but there are usually some available for the friends or supporters of legislators.

So far we have described the use of patronage only to benefit the legislator's district or his political supporters. It may also be used directly to benefit the legislator and his family. Though there has been some decrease in the practice, many states still have a number of commissions with legislative members who are paid substantial salaries. Until dual-officeholding was forbidden in 1951, there were a number of such plums for well-behaved legislators in Connecticut, and the governor sometimes held off making appointments until the end of the session.[10] A survey of the Maryland legislature in 1957 showed that one-fourth of the members were paid by the state: twenty-two were attorneys for the state road commission, while seventeen were insurance agents doing business with the state.[11] In some states it is not uncommon for the administration to arrange for jobs for loyal legislators with firms that have state contracts. In one southern state an undertaking and insurance firm interested in insurance contracts has had as many as fifteen state legislators employed at one time.[12] Until a conflict-of-interest law went into effect in 1961, Kentucky legislators frequently held state jobs, occasionally in addition to jobs with firms having substantial state contracts.

The problem of the legislator who is on the state payroll or who belongs to a business with a state contract, like the problem discussed earlier of the legislator working for a pressure group, is implicit in a situation of part-time legislators with full-time business interests. If there is less danger in a legislator being paid by the governor than by a pressure group, it is only because the governor probably has a clearer concept of the public interest. Some reformers may decry any form of patronage, but there seems to be an important distinction between the legislator who supports the administration to win roads for his county or a judgeship for his political ally and another whose support is given simply to line his own pockets. Whether the legislator serves on a state conservation board at full pay, writes insurance policies in his firm for a state agency, or gets his wife employed as a secretary for a construction firm building a state road, he is being bought. He is responsible not to his conscience, his constituents, or his party, but to his direct or indirect or potential employer—the state.

The Governor and Responsible Government

The legislature in some states is often described as a rubber stamp for the governor, and in some states—though by no means all—the governor's record of legislative accomplishment often seems to bear this out. As the problems of government grow more complex and require the knowledge and skill of experts, is a more independent legislature desirable or even possible? The legislature can take a number of steps to improve its staff and the competence of its members, but it seems necessary for the modern governor to take the initiative in developing programs and to press vigorously for their adoption in the legislature. The object of criticism should not be strong gubernatorial leadership but the techniques through which it is exercised.

Patronage, in the broad sense, can be criticized on several grounds: it may place incompetent men in government, raise the cost of governmental services, and corrupt the legislators who profit directly from it. The fundamental criticism of a governor who uses patronage as the major tool of his legislative leadership is that he is undermining responsible government. The legislator who votes for a bill because the governor has been successful in generating public support for it is acting responsibly; he is responding to public demand. Likewise, in a two-party state, the legislator who votes for an administration bill because the governor is his party's leader is acting responsibly; he realizes that he was elected as a member of the governor's party with at least a general mandate to support the governor. But the legislator who votes for a bill in order to get a contract for the businessman who financed his campaign is not acting responsibly; he has no mandate to trade his vote for favors, and *his constituents almost never know the reason for his vote.*

When the governor dominates a legislature through his use of patronage, he makes a sham of representative government. In such a situation, the legislators are accountable not to the voters but to the governor, and he does not need to persuade them but merely to issue instructions. "The relationship is not subtle; it is direct, brutal, and it is effective." [13] The legislature, which theoretically serves as a check on the governor, can become his pawn.

Patronage is a weapon of governors in all states, but it represents a larger part of their arsenal in most one-party states. We have seen that party unity varies considerably among the two-party states. Where the governor has strong support from the majority party, this is primarily because he and the legislators of his party share common interests: they represent similar groups in the electorate and they both have a stake in a successful administration that can win another term. The voters can judge their record intelligently. Patronage becomes a supplementary tool of gubernatorial leadership. In a competitive two-party state the minority party is strong enough to prevent any long-term executive domination of the legislature. When there are strong parties but divided government, there is no danger of executive domination but a real possibility of deadlock between the two branches of government. Deadlocked government is irresponsible because the voter frequently does not know which party is to blame for inaction or for unwise legislation. In theory divided government produces compromise, but in practice it usually produces either deadlock or trades negotiated in secret and facilitated by the generous use of patronage. Once again the voter is left in the dark.

When a single party dominates, there is the greatest likelihood that the governor will win adoption of his program mainly through patronage. Obviously he can be expected to win a number of votes because legislators are convinced that the legislation is right or has strong public support, but when the going gets rough he cannot rely on party loyalty but must turn to patronage. If the legislature over-represents rural areas, the differences between executive and legislature often can be bridged, if at all, only by patronage. Gubernatorial dominance of the legislative process is most damaging in a one-party state because the voter does not understand how it was achieved; he does not know whether his legislator actually voted for a bill because he thought it was good legislation or because he had been offered some form of patronage.

Gubernatorial domination through patronage in a one-party state is also open to criticism because it usually undermines whatever minority party exists. The governor sometimes finds it easier to buy minority party votes with patronage because those legislators are hungry for benefits for their districts and their supporters. The more patronage they can get, the less incentive they have to gain majority status; the more often they support the governor, the fewer issues their party has for the next campaign. When a recent Kentucky Democratic governor needed Republican votes for his program, he told the Republican members in a caucus that voting support was the price for roads and parks in their districts. If the two-party system is the surest guarantee of responsible government, the sharpest indictment of gubernatorial domination through patronage is that it serves to perpetuate one-party politics.

SIX

POLITICAL RESPONSIBILITY
AND THE LEGISLATURE

Most studies of American legislatures, like those of the French Fourth Republic, center on what is wrong with them. Most observers conclude that few legislatures are doing their job well and that many of the ills of state government result from that fact. The remedy that is prescribed for the legislature usually consists of steps to improve its competence. Legislators should be paid more and should serve a longer time, there should be more adequate staffs and stronger legislative councils, and the legislature should meet longer and more often in order to give more careful study to legislative proposals. Every one of these suggestions is sound, and each would improve the legislative process.

It is the thesis of this book, however, that the legislative process is a political one and that the fundamental weakness of many legislative bodies is a lack of political responsibility. The legislature cannot be separated from its political environment, which is the primary factor determining how power is exercised within it. In a one-party state the legislature is likely to be irresponsible. Power may be widely dispersed among many groups in the legislature or it may be concentrated in the governor's hands. In either case, legislative decisions are likely to be made as a result of deals—among the members, with the governor, or with pressure groups, deals of which the public is ignorant. In a one-party state, legislative candidates often run unopposed; even when there is competition, they do not stand for anything in the public mind. The legislators have no mandate—either for a program or for support of the administration; consequently they are free to make whatever deals are necessary and possible in the state legislature.

A strong two-party state is no guarantee of legislative responsibility. The parties may be so heterogeneous that they stand for nothing and have no reason to maintain unity in the legislature. Legislators with lopsided majorities in their districts may be insensitive to constituents. Gubernatorial control may be so strong that legislators are robots, or the apportionment system may have created a divided government in which deadlock is the norm. Despite these problems, the greatest possibilities for responsible government lie in a two-party system. When there are two parties reasonably competitive in the state and in many districts, each capable of winning full control of the government, each identified with certain policies and programs, the voter has some real choice. He has some opportunity to pick legislators who are likely to support one or another gubernatorial candidate who is advancing a program familiar, at least in broad outlines, to the voter.

Legislatures often fall short of our expectations largely because at any one time such a two-party system can be found operating well in relatively few states. There is hope for a greater number of responsible legislatures, however, because it is possible to forecast a growth of the two-party system. We noted this trend in Chapter II. Republican strongholds have crumbled through the North, and two-party politics has grown strong. The Republicans are making inroads more slowly into the solid Democratic states in the south and border region. Urbanization, population migration, and the fading of political habits and traditions have all contributed to this trend. The trend is developing slowly, almost imperceptibly in a few states. In states like Virginia and

Louisiana, where two-party politics has become a familiar feature of national elections, there are many obstacles to building a state Republican party. In some of these states the minority party is clearly losing ground and the fragmentary Republican gains in the 1950's appear to have been lost. But in the long run, as long as the number of states that are competitive in national politics continues to grow, forces contributing to state two-party systems will continue to mount.

Perhaps better than any other state, California exemplifies the new trend toward two-party politics. For many years California was Republican in its state politics. At times the Republican party was torn by a struggle between progressives and conservatives, each represented by members in the legislature, but in later years the party became more united. The Republicans were so strong and the Democrats so weak that the dominant tone of the legislature was a nonpartisan one. The cross-filing system and the pro-rural apportionment both contributed to Republican dominance and Democratic weakness. Except when the state had a strong governor, pressure groups were unusually effective in the legislature.

California has been engulfed by new citizens, and the traditional political practices have been pushed aside, including the dominant atmosphere of nonpartisan Republicanism. The Democratic party has been rebuilt, the cross-filing system has been abandoned, and there have recently been major revisions in apportionment. The legislature has grown more political, and party lines are beginning to mean something in the roll calls. Spearheading the Democratic rebirth have been the state Democratic Clubs. An outgrowth of the Stevenson clubs, these groups are middle-class, policy-oriented groups with local chapters and a statewide organization. They endorse, with considerable success, selected candidates in the Democratic party. The newer Democratic legislators are often members of the clubs or owe their nomination and election to the clubs. They are sensitive to the views of the clubs, which maintain an active interest in legislative issues. The clubs have provided the base for a program-oriented Democratic party. Younger legislators see more need for effective caucuses and greater party unity in the legislature. The Republicans, in self-defense, have had to strengthen their own organizational unity in the legislature.[1]

What has happened in California can happen, with local variations, in any of the states, but it is most likely in those that are growing and changing, becoming urbanized and industrialized most rapidly. New citizens in these growing states may not conform to the voting traditions of their new community, nor are they likely to vote for a candidate simply because he was born and raised in the town. They are more likely to ask what he stands for, what program his party is pledged to. Urbanization confronts the states with new problems that cannot be solved by outdated methods. Sooner or later the citizens of large urban centers will demand that their interests be adequately represented, not only by a more equitable apportionment, but by legislators who are committed to some program serving urban needs. States that are becoming urban are likely to become two-party states, and sooner or later this change will be felt in the legislatures.

The state legislature offers a fascinating area for analysis to the student who is interested in the political process. Not only are there changes occurring that we know little about, but there are great gaps in our knowledge about the recent past. The existence of fifty legislative systems offers a real challenge to discover meaningful patterns in the wide variety of practices. The careful student has probably noted that many of the examples in this book have been drawn from relatively few states and that on some questions the evidence presented has been thin. The opportunities for study are limitless, and they do not require expensive trips to the far corners of the globe. A few hours or even minutes away from every college campus is a state capital where an experiment in democratic government is being conducted. As V. O. Key has pointed out, many of the states are equal in population and in the scope of government to many foreign countries.[2] Their operations affect American citizens often as vitally as do those of the federal government.

There is occurring today a renaissance in the study of comparative state politics; it should be extended to a thorough examination of the role of parties in government, principally in the legislative branch. This book has served its purpose if it has not only provided some initial insights into legislative politics but has stimulated interests in further exploration.

NOTES

I. Introduction

1. V. O. Key, Jr., *Southern Politics in State and Nation* (New York: Alfred A. Knopf, 1950); *American State Politics: An Introduction* (New York: Alfred A. Knopf, 1956).
2. Belle Zeller, ed., *American State Legislatures* (New York: Thomas Y. Crowell Co., 1954).

II. The Election of Legislators

1. See Austin Ranney and Willmoore Kendall, "The American Party Systems," *American Political Science Review,* XLVIII (1954), 477-485.
2. V. O. Key, Jr., *American State Politics: An Introduction* (New York: Alfred A. Knopf, 1956) pp. 53-57.
3. *Ibid.,* pp. 58-64.
4. *Ibid.,* pp. 64-73.
5. Gordon E. Baker, *Rural Versus Urban Political Power* (New York: Random House Studies in Political Science, 1955) pp. 9-10. This and Baker's other short book, *State Constitutions: Reapportionment* (New York: National Municipal League, 1960) are two of the best brief treatments of the apportionment problem and are the sources of several examples in this chapter. See also: *Compendium on Legislative Apportionment* (New York: National Municipal League, 1960).
6. Baker, *State Constitutions: Reapportionment,* pp. 50-55.
7. Duane Lockard, *New England State Politics* (Princeton: Princeton University Press, 1959) pp. 271-273.
8. For an analysis of the effects of malapportionment in Ohio, see Thomas A. Flinn, "The Outline of Ohio Politics," *Western Political Quarterly,* XIII (1960), 702-721.
9. Lockard, *op. cit.,* pp. 177-189.
10. See *Compendium on Legislative Apportionment.*
11. Baker, *State Constitutions: Reapportionment,* pp. 22-23.
12. Maurice Klain, "A New Look at the Constituencies: The Need for a Recount and a Reappraisal," *American Political Science Review,* XLIX (1955), 1105-1119.

13. George S. Blair, "Cumulative Voting: Patterns of Party Allegiance and Rational Choice in Illinois State Leglislative Contests," *American Political Science Review*, LII (1958), 123-130.
14. These figures were gathered directly from state yearbooks and from: Duane Lockard, *op. cit.*, pp. 56, 99-100, 125, 188, 205, 256; Key, *op. cit.*, p. 190; Leon D. Epstein, *Politics in Wisconsin* (Madison: University of Wisconsin Press, 1958) p. 203; George S. Blair, *Cumulative Voting* (Urbana: University of Illinois Press, 1960) p. 55.
15. Key, *op. cit.*, pp. 181-196.
16. Lockard, *op. cit.*, pp. 188-205.
17. Joseph LaPalombara, *Guide to Michigan Politics* (Bureau of Social and Political Research, Michigan State University, 1960) p. 23.
18. Winston W. Crouch and Dean E. McHenry, *California Government* (Berkeley: University of California Press, 1949) p. 36.
19. Lockard, *op. cit.*, p. 56.
20. See Malcolm E. Jewell, "Party and Primary Competition in Kentucky State Legislative Races," *Kentucky Law Journal*, XLVIII (1960), 517-535.
21. Key, *op. cit.*, pp. 171-181.
22. Key, *op. cit.*, p. 178.
23. Lockard, *op. cit.*, pp. 23, 54.
24. Allan P. Sindler, *Huey Long's Louisiana* (Baltimore: The Johns Hopkins Press, 1956) pp. 273-282.

III. Voting Alignments in the Legislature

1. Belle Zeller, ed., *American State Legislatures* (New York: Thomas Y. Crowell Co., 1954) pp. 192-193.
2. *Congressional Quarterly Almanac*, 1955-1960 (Washington: Congressional Quarterly, Inc.)
3. V. O. Key, Jr., *Southern Politics in State and Nation* (New York: Alfred A. Knopf, 1950) p. 370.
4. Julius Turner, *Party and Constituency: Pressures on Congress* (Baltimore: Johns Hopkins Press, 1952) p. 24.
5. It should be noted that, while all of the studies summarized in Table 3 exclude unanimous roll calls, some also exclude those with 10 per cent or less of the members (or in some cases of both parties) voting in the minority. This can make a significant difference in the

statistics for a state like Illinois where this category makes up about one-sixth of the roll calls. The figures in Table 3 are based on my own studies and on the following sources: Duane Lockard, *New England State Politics* (Princeton: Princeton University Press, 1959); Duane Lockard, "Legislative Politics in Connecticut," *American Political Science Review*, XLVIII (1954), 166-173; William J. Keefe, "Parties, Partisanship and Public Policy in the Pennsylvania Legislature," *American Political Science Review*, XLVIII (1954), 450-464; Thomas A. Flinn, "The Outline of Ohio Politics," *Western Political Quarterly*, XIII (1960), 702-721; David R. Derge, "Urban-Rural Relationships in the Illinois General Assembly, 1949-1957" (Paper presented at the 1958 meeting of the Midwest Conference of Political Scientists); Dean R. Cresap, *Party Politics in The Golden State* (Los Angeles: The Haynes Foundation, 1954) p. 57; William Buchanan, unpublished manuscript on California; William C. Johnson, "The Political Party System in the 1959-1960 California Legislature," (Unpublished M. A. thesis, University of California, 1960) p. 77. In several cases additional information has been provided directly by these writers. See also my "Party Voting in American State Legislatures," *American Political Science Review*, XLIX (1955), 773-791.

6. Lockard, *New England States Politics*, p. 151.

7. Warren Moscow, *Politics in the Empire State* (New York: Alfred A. Knopf, 1948) pp. 175-176.

8. Ralph A. Straetz and Frank J. Munger, *New York Politics* (New York: New York University Press, 1960) p. 61.

9. Daniel M. Ogden, Jr., and Hugh A. Bone, *Washington Politics* (New York: New York University Press, 1960) p. 21.

10. Cresap, *op. cit.*, p. 61; Johnson, *op. cit.*

11. John G. Grumm, "Party Responsibility in the Kansas Legislature" (Paper presented at the Wichita Conference on Politics, April 10, 1959). Samuel C. Patterson, "The Role of the Deviant in the State Legislative System," *Western Political Quarterly*, XIV (1961), 460-472.

12. Robert H. Salisbury, "Missouri Politics and State Political Systems" (Bureau of Government Research, University of Missouri, 1959).

13. William J. Keefe, "Comparative Study of the Role of

Political Parties in State Legislatures," *Western Political Quarterly*, IX (1956), 726-742. See also Jewell, *op. cit.*, 788-790.

14. David R. Derge, "Metropolitan and Outstate Alignments in Illinois and Missouri Legislative Delegations," *American Political Science Review*, LII (1958), 1051-1065. Flinn, *op. cit.*, pp. 715-720.

15. Zeller, *op. cit.*, pp. 206-208.

16. Lockard, *New England State Politics*, pp. 38-39.

17. *Compendium on Legislative Apportionment* (New York: National Municipal League, 1960). There are many examples of urban-rural differences on specific issues cited in this volume.

18. Loren P. Beth and William C. Havard, "Committee Stacking and Political Power in Florida," *Journal of Politics*, XXIII (1961), 57-83.

19. Zeller, *op. cit.*, p. 209.

20. Havens measured the significance of urban-rural voting by using the Chi-square test with a level of significance of .05. Murray C. Havens, *City versus Farm?* (Bureau of Public Administration, University of Alabama, 1957).

21. Duncan MacRae, Jr., "The Relation Between Roll Call Votes and Constituencies in the Massachusetts House of Representatives," *American Political Science Review*, XLVI (1952), 1046-1055; Thomas R. Dye, "A Comparison of Constituency Influences in the Upper and Lower Chambers of a State Legislature," *Western Political Quarterly*, XIV (1961), 473-480; Patterson, *op. cit.*

22. Belle Zeller, "Regulation of Pressure Groups and Lobbyists," *Annals of the American Academy of Political and Social Science*, Vol. 319 (1958), p. 95.

23. David B. Truman, *The Governmental Process* (New York: Alfred A. Knopf, 1953) p. 321.

24. John C. Wahlke and others, "American State Legislators' Role Orientations Toward Pressure Groups," *Journal of Politics*, XXII (1960), 203-227. Oliver Garceau and Corinne Silverman, "A Pressure Group and the Pressured: A Case Report," *American Political Science Review* XLVIII (1954), 672-691.

25. Zeller, *American State Legislatures*, pp. 204-209.

IV. Political Organization of the Legislature

1. *Book of the States, 1960-61* (Chicago: Council of State Governments, 1960) pp. 508-560.

2. An excellent description of the presiding officer in state legislatures is: Eugene C. Lee, *The Presiding Officer and Rules Committee in Legislatures of the United States* (Berkeley: Bureau of Public Administration, University of California, 1952).

3. Austin Ranney, *Illinois Politics* (New York: New York University Press, 1960) p. 28. Lee, *op. cit.*, pp. 29, 37.

4. Loren P. Beth and William C. Havard, "Committee Stacking and Political Power in Florida," *Journal of Politics*, XXIII (1961), 65.

5. *Time*, May 5, 1961.

6. *New York Times*, June 6, 23, 27, July 2, 1959.

7. *Book of the States, 1960-61*, p. 45.

8. Thomas Page, *Legislative Apportionment in Kansas* (Lawrence: Bureau of Government Research, University of Kansas, 1952) p. 119.

9. Lee, *op. cit.*, pp. 42-47.

10. *Ibid.*, pp. 17-18.

11. *Book of the States, 1960-61*, pp. 46-47.

12. W. F. Willoughby, *Principles of Legislative Organization and Administration* (Washington: Brookings Institution, 1934) p. 622.

13. Belle Zeller, ed., *American State Legislatures* (New York: Thomas Y. Crowell Co., 1954) p. 195.

14. Hallie Farmer, *The Legislative Process in Alabama* (Bureau of Public Administration, University of Alabama, 1949) pp. 189-191.

15. Lee, *op. cit.*, pp. 19, 23, 34-36.

16. Farmer, *op. cit.*, pp. 64-65, 160-161.

17. Gilbert Y. Steiner and Samuel K. Gove, *Legislative Politics in Illinois* (Urbana: University of Illinois Press, 1960) pp. 12-13.

18. Duane Lockard, *New England State Politics* (Princeton: Princeton University Press, 1959) pp. 116, 218.

19. William J. Siffin, *The Legislative Council in the American States* (Bloomington: Indiana University Press, 1959).

20. Zeller, *op. cit.*, pp. 195-196, 203-210.

21. *Ibid.*, p. 207.

22. "Where Caucus Is Still King," *National Municipal Review*, XXXIX (1950), 119-120. *New York Times*, Oct. 17, 1957, Jan. 15, 1958.

23. Lockard, *op. cit.*, pp. 281-282.

24. Winston W. Crouch and Dean E. McHenry, *California Government* (Berkeley: University of California Press,

1949) p. 86. Dean R. Cresap, *Party Politics in the Golden State* (Los Angeles: The Haynes Foundation, 1954) pp. 52-53. William C. Johnson, "The Political Party System in the 1959-1960 California Legislature" (Unpublished M. A. thesis, University of California, 1960) pp. 23, 103-104.

25. Zeller, *op. cit.*, p. 210.
26. *Ibid.*, pp. 68-69.
27. Robert F. Karsch, *The Standing Committees of the Missouri General Assembly* (Columbia: Bureau of Government Research, University of Missouri, 1959) pp. 17-18.
28. Steiner and Gove, *op. cit.*, pp. 78-81.
29. Johnson, *op. cit.*, pp. 40-43.
30. G. Theodore Mitau, *Politics in Minnesota* (Minneapolis: University of Minnesota Press, 1960) pp. 59-62.
31. Beth and Havard, *op. cit.*
32. Lockard, *op. cit.*, p. 149.
33. Steiner and Gove, *op. cit.*, pp. 17-18.
34. *Ibid.*, pp. 58-83.

V. The Governor as a Legislator

1. Coleman B. Ransone, Jr., *The Office of Governor in the United States* (University, Ala.: University of Alabama Press, 1956) pp. 176-179. See also his *The Office of Governor in the South* (Bureau of Public Administration, University of Alabama, 1951) pp. 72-74. These excellent volumes are the two best sources of information on the governor as a legislative leader.
2. Frank W. Prescott, "The Executive Veto in American States," *Western Political Quarterly*, III (1950), 97-111.
3. Ransone, *The Office of Governor in the United States*, pp. 182-184.
4. *Book of the States, 1960-61* (Chicago: Council of State Governments, 1960) p. 51.
5. Ransone, *The Office of Governor in the United States*, pp. 166-169.
6. Hallie Farmer, *The Legislative Process in Alabama* (Bureau of Public Administration, University of Alabama, 1949) pp. 185-188.
7. Warren Moscow, *Politics in the Empire State* (New York: Alfred A. Knopf, 1948) pp. 174-175.
8. Duane Lockard, *New England State Politics* (Princeton: Princeton University Press, 1959) pp. 300-302.

9. See Ransone, *The Office of Governor in the South*, pp. 88-96.
10. Lockard, *op. cit.*, p. 298.
11. *Washington Post and Times Herald*, June 24, 1958.
12. Ransone, *The Office of Governor in the South*, pp. 95-96.
13. Robert Highsaw, "Southern Governor—Challenge to the Strong Executive Theme," *Public Administration Review*, XIX (1959), 9.

VI. *Political Responsibility and the Legislature*

1. William C. Johnson, "The Political Party System in the 1959-1960 California Legislature" (Unpublished M. A. thesis, University of California, 1960); Francis Carney, *The Rise of the Democratic Clubs in California* (New York: Henry Holt and Co., 1958).
2. V. O. Key, Jr., *American State Politics: An Introduction* (New York: Alfred A. Knopf, 1956) preface.

SELECTED BIBLIOGRAPHY

There are relatively few studies available dealing with state legislatures, particularly if we limit the selection to modern studies that include the political realities of the legislative process. Most of these have already been mentioned in the notes. The best single study is that made by a committee of the American Political Science Association and edited by Belle Zeller, *American State Legislatures* (New York: Thomas Y. Crowell Co., 1954). It is comprehensive, with figures showing the number of states following various practices, and it describes some of the political factors involved in legislatures.

There have been several general books on the legislative process that give some attention to the states, but most deal with formal aspects of legislatures (rules, procedures, mechanics) rather than political aspects, and most are out of date. One of the more recent of these is Harvey Walker, *The Legislative Process* (New York: Ronald Press, 1948). Textbooks on state government normally have a chapter or two on legislatures, but these also tend to stress the formalities of the legislative process. A valuable source of current information on various state legislatures is the biennial *Book of the States* (Chicago: Council of State Governments), which has tables covering such matters as the number of committees, party division, veto requirements, and the procedure for passing bills.

There is a growing body of literature on legislative behavior. These studies focus on the legislators as individual actors, their roles, their relations with other legislators and lobbyists, their concepts of the legislative process. A number of examples of these studies, dealing with state legislatures, Congress, and some foreign legislatures, are found in a book of readings edited by John C. Wahlke and Heinz Eulau, *Legislative Behavior* (Glencoe, Ill.: The Free Press, 1959). The results of a comparative behavioral analysis of four state legislatures will appear in a forthcoming book by William Buchanan, Heinz Eulau, LeRoy C. Ferguson, and John C. Wahlke. This is an area of growing interest to scholars, and their work has been reported in a number of recent journal articles. Interested students might look at articles by Wilder Crane, Jr., Duncan

MacRae, Jr., Corinne Silverman, and Samuel C. Patterson, for example.

There are abundant articles and monographs on the legislative apportionment problems of individual states. The best brief treatment of the question can be found in two studies by Gordon E. Baker, *Rural Versus Urban Political Power* (New York: Random House Studies in Political Science, 1955) and *State Constitutions: Reapportionment* (New York: National Municipal League, 1960). The National Municipal League in 1960 published a very useful state-by-state *Compendium on Legislative Apportionment*, which is being updated to include 1960 census figures and 1961 apportionment laws. A number of aspects of the problem are studied in a somewhat outdated volume, "Legislative Reapportionment," *Law and Contemporary Problems*, XVII (Spring, 1952).

There have been a number of studies of roll call voting in the legislatures, most of which were mentioned in the notes for Chapter Three; some are summarized in William J. Keefe's article "Comparative Study of the Role of Political Parties in State Legislatures," *Western Political Quarterly*, IX (Sept. 1956), 726-742. Among the writers who have done the most significant work in this area are Keefe, David R. Derge, Duncan MacRae, Jr., and Duane Lockard.

The best chapters on the legislative role of the governor are found in two volumes by Coleman B. Ransone, Jr., *The Office of Governor in the United States* (University, Ala.: University of Alabama Press, 1956) and *The Office of Governor in the South* (Bureau of Public Administration, University of Alabama, 1951). See also Robert Highsaw, "Southern Governor—Challenge to the Strong Executive Theme," *Public Administration Review*, XIX (1959), 7-11.

There are numerous books and monographs concerning the legislative process in individual states. Many of these deal almost exclusively with rules and procedures; by and large they provide little understanding of the political process in the legislature. A notable exception, which fulfills the promise in its title, is Gilbert Y. Steiner and Samuel K. Gove, *Legislative Politics in Illinois* (Urbana: University of Illinois Press, 1960). Others that provide a better-than-average picture of the legislative process are: Hallie Farmer, *The Legislative Process in Alabama* (Bureau of Public Administration, University of Alabama, 1949); C. C. Young, *The Legislature of*

California (San Francisco: The Commonwealth Club of California, 1943); Joseph A. Beek, *The California Legislature* (Sacramento: State Printing Office, 1957); *The Legislative Process in Kentucky* (Frankfort: Legislative Research Commission, 1955). Note also two of the volumes in the Eagleton Institute Case Studies in Practical Politics: Duane Lockard, *Connecticut's Challenge Primary: A Study in Legislative Politics*, and Gordon E. Baker, *The Politics of Reapportionment in Washington State* (Holt, Rinehart, and Winston, 1959 and 1960).

The field of comparative state politics is rapidly growing, and some of the books in this field devote considerable attention to political aspects of the legislature. The best examples are Duane Lockard, *New England State Politics* (Princeton: Princeton University Press, 1959) and V. O. Key, Jr., *American State Politics: An Introduction* (New York: Alfred A. Knopf, 1956). Others are: Warren Moscow, *Politics in the Empire State* (New York: Alfred A. Knopf, 1948); Ralph A. Straetz and Frank J. Munger, *New York Politics* (New York: New York University Press, 1960); Donald R. Cresap, *Party Politics in the Golden State* (Los Angeles: The Haynes Foundation, 1954); G. Theodore Mitau, *Politics in Minnesota* (Minneapolis: University of Minnesota Press, 1960); Leon D. Epstein, *Politics in Wisconsin* (Madison: University of Wisconsin Press, 1958); Daniel M. Ogden, Jr., and Hugh A. Bone, *Washington Politics* (New York: New York University Press, 1960).

For a more comprehensive bibliography on state legislatures, see Norman Meller, "Legislative Behavior Research," *Western Political Quarterly*, XIII (March, 1960), pp. 131-153.

INDEX